GENTLE PARENTING

A BEGINNERS BOOK FOR RAISING CHILDREN WITH LOVE, RESPECT, AND POSITIVE DISCIPLINE

ELIZABETH RAY

© Copyright 2021 —All rights reserved.

It is not legal to reproduce, duplicate, or transmit any part of this document in either electronic means or in printed format. Recording of this publication is strictly prohibited and any storage of this document is not allowed unless with written permission from the publisher except for the use of brief quotations in a book review.

CONTENTS

Introduction	v
1. The Four Major Parenting Styles	1
2. Gentle and Respectful Parenting	15
3. Everything Starts with You	25
4. Model Positive Discipline	35
5. Create the Environment for Success	49
6. Setting Kind and Firm Limits	71
7. Respond to Misbehavior	83
8. Love and Logic Consequences	99
9. Apply Respectful Discipline Methods	109
10. From Complaining to Contributing	117
Afterword	123

SPECIAL BONUS!

Want This Bonus Book for Free?

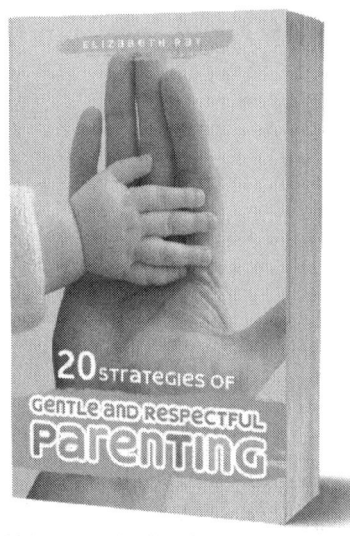

Get **FREE**, Unlimited access to it and all of my new books by joining the Fan Base!

Scan W/ Your Camera to Join!

INTRODUCTION

As soon as a couple learns that they're going to have a baby, it can be said that the journey of parenting has started already. At this point, the thought of having a beautiful baby to love and cherish as well as the idea of becoming a parent is one that can be very exciting. We don't necessarily pay attention to the actual workings of parenting that child just yet. When we finally hold our children in our arms, we begin to ask questions ranging from how to feed them to how to comfort them to how to raise them. Sadly, babies don't come with user manuals and just because we become parents does not mean that we'll naturally excel at it. In such situations, it is common to fall back on the parenting style that we were also raised with. However, not all parenting styles are beneficial in the real sense and we'd rather create a relationship with open lines of communication where our kids can grow confidently and independently. Now the goal becomes mutually respecting our children and strengthening our connection with them.

Respectful and gentle parenting basically involves seeing our children as whole people right from when they are born and treating them with the same respect we'd give to any other person. Unfortunately, our society frequently discriminates against children and treats them like they are inferior which should not be so. When dealing with other adults, we never have to remind ourselves that they should be treated with respect—why then do we have to do so with children? Respecting children implies that we would treat them the same way we would treat an adult that would not be seen as offensive. Even though we need to care, guide, and protect them, we can always do this with respect as well. When we do this, we trust that our children can grow and learn naturally when we create a conducive environment for them.

Respectful parenting involves acknowledging the emotions of our children and not just discarding them as childish displays. This way, we build our interest in them and also encourage their emotional development. There are so many great results that we can achieve as parents when we take note of our children's emotions without belittling them or judging them. Responding with love and understanding helps your child to see you as a safe harbor where they can always run to when they need to express their feelings.

This method of child raising can be tricky for many parents today as many of us were brought up in families where obedience was of greater importance than a loving relationship. Many of us were raised believing that children were inferior and their opinions don't matter, and we can get trapped in these concepts as well. This isn't because we don't want the best for our children but because it might feel like the best parenting method, especially as those approaches can be effective in the short-term. However, the long-term effects of this should be considered too. Do you want your child to be able to approach you when they do something wrong, or do you want them to hide their mistakes out of fear? Do we want children who can speak up courageously or those that will blindly obey anything they are told? Would you rather provide your child with needed skills to take charge of his or her life or do you want to lead and control them? At first, it may seem like this method of raising our children respectfully is a permissive approach that allows them to have free reign but scientifically, it has been proven to be more effective in raising children than regular traditional methods. It is up to us as parents to choose the best method of parenting that will help our children grow to be loving, respectful, disciplined, and well-rounded people.

In this book, we take an in-depth look into major aspects of child upbringing along with ways we can make use of positive and respectful discipline to raise our children. It contains valuable information on everything you need to know about child development and how you can raise kids that are happy and well-behaved with respect and love. When your child misbehaves, how do you react to them? It can be tempting to deal out punitive actions in order to discourage said behavior but in this book, we take a look at better and healthier ways parents can respond. We also consider the different kinds of parenting styles, the use of consequences, how we can be role models for our children—these and much more are thoroughly covered in this book. Whether you are a parent, babysitter, aunt, or uncle, the helpful nuggets contained in this book are sure to help you create a deeper and more meaningful relationship with your child. Dive in now and get all the tools you need to begin your journey to raising well-disciplined kids with love and respect!

1

THE FOUR MAJOR PARENTING STYLES

There is no denying that children are a blessing. These wonderful gifts are extensions of ourselves in some ways and watching as they grow from infancy can be intriguing to say the least. This period of time will definitely be filled with some of the most beautiful memories you'll ever make. Along that line however, there will come a point where you'll have to make some important decisions. These decisions will go a long way in shaping your young one's life and therefore require careful consideration. One such decision is deciding how you're going to raise your child. Whether as a single parent or with a partner, choosing a particular parenting style can be a challenging task for many. Although parenting styles may have some variations from each person to the next, there are some main categories that have been noted over the years. They are authoritarian, authoritative, permissive, and neglectful. Each of these styles have peculiar features or characteristics that distinguish them from one another. In this chapter, we will take a look at each of them and see how they affect a child's upbringing.

The Authoritarian Style of Parenting

This kind of parenting style is generally seen as being too strict and presents high demands from the parents but low responsiveness. In this kind of setting, children are expected to stick to the rules laid out by their parents with no complaints made or questions asked. They typically have a lot of demands placed on them by parents who give little to no feedback or proper nurturing. The authoritarian parenting style on its own gives little room for open communication and mistakes will often result in harsh punishments. Corporal punishments and yelling are commonplace and it's not farfetched to say that children brought up with this style will feel more like subjects than members of a family. Authoritarian parents are more concerned about the fancy "parent" tag than they are about creating a positive and nurturing environment for their kids. To them, children should only be seen, and not heard. They don't see a need to have a fun conversation with their children or find out what's going on in their lives—they just have to be obeyed with no explanations.

Mindy, now 36, says, "Even while I was in college, my mum still largely determined how I spent the money I made working part time—I could not buy myself anything without her approval. I was only allowed to go to school, the restaurant where I worked, and back home. Relationships were not allowed, and she'd yell at me if I stayed out a minute past the time she expected me back home. Friends were off limits, and I was expected to graduate with a First Class Honors or nothing!" Parents who use the authoritarian parenting style do not usually display emotions or affection and can get very critical if their children do not meet the standards or expectations they have set. They lay down a whole lot of rules and sometimes will manage all areas of their children's lives and actions as well. Rather than praise their kids and encourage them, there's a higher chance of them yelling at them instead.

Authoritarian parents can be very distrusting and are always doubtful that their children will make the right choices. The interesting fact about this is that they rarely give their kids the chance to show good behavior. Instead of letting their kids make their own decisions and face the natural consequences, they hover around them to make sure that they make no mistakes.

Are You an Authoritarian Parent?

Have you set strict rules for your kids without giving any explanation for the reason why they exist in the first place?

Do you expect your children to follow all rules to the letter without asking any questions? How often do you have to respond with ...*because I said so!*?

When your children question your rules or break them, do you resort to yelling and swift punishments? Also ask yourself:

- Are your children free to express themselves and speak freely around you?
- How close are you to your children physically and emotionally?
- Do you present your children with very limited choices?

Effects of The Authoritarian Parenting Style on Children

Aside from displaying aggressiveness outside the home, children can also be socially awkward and find it hard to make decisions on their own.

As they are rarely allowed to socialize, children become socially incompetent and will handle social situations with difficulty. Other effects include:

- They may be excessively shy around other people or show signs of fearfulness.
- They typically suffer from anxiety and depression but will conform to rules and standards easily.
- They link success and being obedient with love.
- Children have low self-esteem, judge characters poorly and may rebel against authority figures at an older age.
- Children can get very resentful and find it hard to keep their anger in check.
- They will model this same behavior with peers and their future children as well.
- They cannot think on their own and develop a fear of failing at anything.
- Children raised this way may end up becoming permissive parents to their own children.

The Authoritative Style of Parenting

This style of parenting is generally seen as the best kind because it balances independence and structure. This in turn allows children to explore their abilities as much as they want to and also grow within healthy boundaries. Authoritative parenting can be considered as a middle ground of parenting styles as it involves respecting every child's individual personality. Along with a loving relationship, it also promotes intimacy and respect. Although parents who make use of this parenting style will set strict standards for their children to abide by, they will also provide an environment that will give them proper support. The authoritative parenting style is firm, but it is also nurturing as children are allowed to make mistakes without judgement in a setting that provides needed guidance. Parents will be assertive but will not try to restrict their children or intrude into their affairs. While they also have high expectations of their children, the guidance and support they give them encourages a positive outcome.

Rules are set just like other parenting styles but with careful explanation and fair expectations. In the event of mistakes, consistent discipline is offered but parents help their kids to see why they are getting disciplined and ways to avoid such later on. "My mom and dad provided me with the best childhood ever," Michael says. "I was never afraid to ask questions and they were always ready to talk to me. They made their expectations of me very clear and would always ask for my opinion on matters. Whenever I broke a rule, they enforced positive discipline methods and they would always let me know why I had to be disciplined." Authoritative parents are concerned with helping their children become cooperative, assertive, self-regulated, and socially responsible.

There is a high presence of flexibility in this parenting style and so it might not be the same in every household as all children are different. For example, if you have a toddler who's refusing to eat dinner, the authoritative parenting style involves using the chance to explain that this is the right time to eat. The toddler may not be expected to wipe the plate clean but he or she may be expected to eat the served meal with the knowledge that there will be no different food until another snack or mealtime. Even if the child begins to throw tantrums or whines, the rule stands and will be enforced.

Are You an Authoritative Parent?

Signs that you're an authoritative parent vary, but generally:

- Are you always ready to listen to your children and provide needed assistance and guidance?
- Are your children allowed to share their thoughts and opinions?
- Do you encourage your children to discuss their options with you?
- Do you see a need to build and maintain a positive relationship with your children?
- Are rules consistently enforced with your children?
- Are you available to give your children needed counsel and encouragement when they go through challenges?
- Do you provide adequate support for your kids along with the expectations you have of them?

Effects of The Authoritative Parenting Style on Children

- Children have more self-confidence and are comfortable in their capability to learn new things.
- They are able to control their emotions effectively and can also regulate them.
- Children perform excellently in their academics as they are given constant support and care by their parents.
- They typically grow to be self-aware adults with clear understanding of their self-worth.
- Children learn how to balance all aspects of their lives and live harmoniously with ease.
- Children raised with this parenting style have better social competence and will be more socially active.
- They have good EQ and IQ qualities which promote general life balance.

The Permissive Style of Parenting

While the authoritarian style involves setting strict rules for children to follow, the permissive parenting style is at the extreme other end of the spectrum. In this setting, children are allowed to do just what they want, and rules or structures are rarely put in place to avoid upsetting or disappointing the child. Parents can be seen as indulgent, and the style is characterized by high responsiveness levels but low expectations. As opposed to hovering over every move their children make, permissive parents will be very lax and will make little to no effort to keep their kids disciplined or controlled.

There are few expectations, demands, or rules and children

are seen as equals more than anything else. Permissive parents are more concerned with being more of friends or peers to their children and will quickly give in to their wants. This situation requires very little of the children and parents find it hard to say "no" to avoid confrontation. These parents believe that "kids will be kids" and are reluctant to impose any kind of limits at all on them. Jade, 24, has this to say: "Growing up, my parents gave me free rein to do whatever I pleased. Many other adults believed they were too easy on me. I can hardly remember a time when my parents turned down any of my requests or punished me for breaking any rule. They didn't demand too much of me and they were incredibly permissive." Instead of making use of expectations and setting boundaries, permissive parents prefer to use bribery and give gifts as parenting tools.

Even though permissive parents can be very loving and warm, they are very lenient and do not require their children to act maturely or exercise self-control. In matters like TV watching, homework, and mealtimes, children are given the freedom to do as they please.

Are You A Permissive Parent?

- Do you put more emphasis on the freedom your children have than on responsibility?
- When your children break rules, are there any consequences that you enforce?
- Have you set consistent behavior standards and rules for your children?
- In the child-parent relationship, are you seen more as a friend than as a parental figure?

- Do you have to make use of bribes in order to get your children to behave accordingly?
- Is there a carefully laid out structure or schedule for your children?
- Is it clear to your children that they need to be responsible and exhibit good manners?

Effects of The Permissive Parenting Style on Children

- Children have difficulty with solving problems and making decisions as they are not used to guidelines or rules.
- They will be unable to manage their habits or time due to the absence of a proper structure in the home.
- Children of permissive parents may engage in substance use and have a higher chance of becoming delinquents.
- As they aren't shown the best ways to tackle their emotions effectively, they may show more signs of aggression and be less understanding emotionally.
- These children do not strive towards anything as their parents expect little or nothing from them. As a result, they may record low achievements in many areas of their lives.

The Neglectful Style of Parenting

Also known as the uninvolved parenting style, this is marked by low responsiveness and low expectations as well. Certain times, parents like this provide for their kids' basic needs but do not show any concern for them. Children may be given clothing, shelter, and food but zero affection or guidance. In other situations, parents may become neglectful and ignore the simplest needs of their children. Neglectful parents interact with their children with minimal effort or not at all. They hardly partake in their children's events or activities and are not interested in forming any kind of emotional bond with them. In contrast to overprotecting their children, they outrightly distance themselves and are rarely available for long interactions. Parents who are uninvolved respond poorly to their children's needs and do not provide the needed emotional support.

"I rarely ever saw my parents while growing up. They were always too busy to take time out for me. I could always stay out as long as I wanted and there was never anyone waiting to ask me where I had been or how my day went. They missed parent-teacher meetings, graduations and many events that were memorable for me. My feelings and emotions were never addressed and all I had to do was stay out of their way at all times," says Bill.

Most times, uninvolved parents were also raised by similar parents and may begin to repeat these same patterns. Other times, people with this parenting style might be so caught up with their own affairs and lives that there is no room to interact with their kids. In some other cases, parents are so concerned with their own problems that they do not realize their level of detachment towards their children.

Are You A Neglectful or Uninvolved Parent?

- How often do you know the people your children are with or where they are?
- Do you ever ask your children what is going on in their lives and how they are doing?
- Are you emotionally distant from your children?
- How much supervision do you give to your children? The barest minimum, or none at all?
- Do you regularly attend school events and other important events that concern your children?
- Do you show your kids little affection, warmth, and love?
- Do you have little or no behavioral expectations for your children?

Effects of The Neglectful or Uninvolved Parenting Style on Children

- Children raised this way are fearful of becoming dependent on other people.
- Children will likely find it hard to form emotional bonds later in life.
- As they do not get the right amount of attention and affection, they can have low self-esteem and become emotionally needy.
- Uninvolved parents hardly communicate with their children and so they may grow up having problems with social interactions.
- Children have a higher chance of engaging in substance abuse.

- There is a tendency to display more delinquency during the adolescent stage in children raised by uninvolved parents.

Each parenting style is linked with different outcomes in children but factors like social influences, culture, children's temperament, and the way they perceive parental treatment also matter. You may not perfectly fit into any of these styles at all times, and your parenting style may change depending on the specific situation. This is normal and many other parents tend to do this as well. In situations where you use more of one style while your partner uses another, it is best to examine how you both respond to your kids and develop a consistent means of discipline and parenting. To raise confident, resilient, and emotionally healthy children, there is a need for love, structure, support, guidance, discipline, and warmth from trusted adults.

In the absence of appropriate discipline methods, children can end up becoming too relaxed and may even break rules simply for the fun of it. No doubt, discipline is important for any growing child. In the next chapter, we will take a look at positive discipline and its advantages over other traditional parenting methods.

Chapter Summary

- The authoritarian style of parenting is marked by high demands from parents but low responsiveness.
- The authoritative style of parenting balances structure and independence and is generally seen as the best kind.
- The permissive parenting style can be seen as lax with little to no rules or structures put in place.
- The neglectful or uninvolved parenting style is characterized by parents having low responsiveness and low expectations for their children as well.

In the next chapter you will learn the difference between positive discipline parenting and traditional methods as well as information about Adler's principle of behavior influence.

2

GENTLE AND RESPECTFUL PARENTING

IN SIMPLE TERMS, DISCIPLINE IS A WAY BY WHICH children are taught to correct their misbehavior. It involves showing children how to learn from their actions and teaching them to make better choices next time. Discipline is sometimes confused with punishment—however, while punishment involves controlling a child, positive discipline is concerned with teaching him or her to control themselves. What does discipline mean to you and how effective have your methods been so far? Are there things you should let go of? Are there new tricks for you to try? Positive discipline is built on empathy and a respectful relationship between the child and the adult. This style of parenting is concerned with giving children freedom within limits and encourages parents to respond to their children, instead of reacting to them. Positive discipline helps kids to learn valuable lessons rather than simply being obedient and is more effective than traditional methods of discipline in the long term.

Positive discipline is a parenting method that is guided by 5 main principles:

- It is firm but also kind, encouraging, and respectful.
- It promotes connection and helps children to feel significant and have a sense of belonging.
- Its effects are long lasting, and it has positive long-term results for child upbringing.
- It motivates children to discover their capabilities and use their energy constructively.
- It teaches children vital life and social skills that help to build good character.

The basic idea of positive discipline is that there are no such thing as bad children, just bad behavior. As parents, recognizing that our children are only misbehaving but are not inherently bad will make it easier for things to fall into place. Let's say your child hits one of his or her peers and you start to wonder if they have a tendency to be mean to others. Calling him or her naughty or bad will only help to reinforce that negative image. On the contrary, it could be that something in his or her environment is stressing them out and causing them to act badly. Accepting that the behavior was bad and not the child in question will make it easier for you to teach them. You could tell the child their behavior wasn't the best and that they should never hit their friends instead of associating their bad behavior with their personalities.

Positive discipline requires free flow of communication as parents need to take out the time to carefully explain things to their children. This technique leaves room for parents to encourage good behavior and discourage those that need to be stopped. Regardless of the outcome you want in your child's behavior, discipline should be carried out while maintaining a respectful and positive relationship with them. With parents who are authoritarian or overly critical of their children, high emphasis is placed on pinpointing what is done wrong. On the other hand, positive discipline encourages parents to show their children how to make necessary adjustments instead of highlighting what they did wrongly. If you catch your child just after doing something inappropriate, your go-to may be to instruct them not to repeat the action and leave it at that. However, explaining that they misbehaved and telling them how to set things right will be more beneficial. For instance, you could say something like "We shouldn't hit our friends, hitting hurts! Let's see how she's doing. Is she alright or hurt?" This way, the child learns to distinguish proper from improper behavior and how to make amends for bad actions as well.

Children are very interesting little beings and even when they behave wrongly, there are times when they feel justified and believe they are right. Many of us can attest to how frustrating it can be when children remain adamant and insist that their wrong behavior isn't such a big deal. From statements like "He started it," "She didn't want to share with me" and so on, it can be tasking to remain cool and collected. However, arguing back is never an option and parents need to exercise patience and repeat what has been said kindly, but firmly. Careful not to raise your voice or lose your temper, slowly repeat the reason why their improper behavior cannot be excused to them. Empathy also goes a long way in situations like this and the battle can be half-won by simply acknowledging their grievances.

Oftentimes when children show inappropriate behavior, it is because they believe their misbehavior will help them to get a particular result. As parents, the task becomes using this unpleasant behavior as a teaching medium to show them how they have misbehaved and better alternatives to their actions.

Doing this will keep them from seeing misbehavior as a tool that they can make use of when they want to get certain things. Avoid launching into a lecture with them though—it is best to use past behavior and significant examples to drive home your point. If you have ever spent time with children, you will know that they like to test limits and find loopholes where possible. Marcus says, "My daughter, Kayla would expect us to bend the rules we set for her at certain times. If we decided to relax a particular rule just a bit for certain reasons, she'd try to get us to close our eyes toward other ones as well. It was tricky to strike a balance with these rules for her but eventually, we had to put our foot down."

Another aspect of positive discipline is the statement of facts or use of single-word questions and reminders. Doing this has been proven to be more effective than the traditional method of demanding compliance or just throwing orders around. Let's use an example to highlight this point—imagine you have a 5-year-old who typically leaves his toys lying all around after playtime. While it may work sometimes, barking at him to pick up the toys might lead to him asking you to do it instead, saying "no" outrightly, or plainly ignoring you. It would shock you to know that simply saying "toys" in a casual and normal tone might give the desired effects. Instead of shouting orders at children, using a single word in a friendly tone will likely get the job done faster and with less back and forth. You can also ask a question like "Where do we put our toys after playing with them?" rather than "Get your toys back into the box immediately!"

Remember that positive discipline involves mutual respect and regular communication so barking orders at children will only make things tougher. We've all been there—there are days when we just do not have the energy or patience to deal with children's misbehavior and end up dishing out punishments. As most of us were raised using traditional methods also, we have become used to these methods and really do not know any better. However, this cycle does not have to be continued and by paying needed attention to our children's psychological development, we can be even better parents. If you're reading this book, you have taken the first step in learning how to stop equating discipline with punishment and in time, you'll be able to understand the reasons behind your child's behaviors. Learn to discuss your child's needs and feelings as well as yours with them and come up with a mutually acceptable solution together. Write down each of these ideas and then decide on the ones you'd like to follow up on to create a warm and nurturing atmosphere for your kids.

As adults, we might be conscious of the fact that each of our actions have a particular consequence—this is the natural order of things and there is really no use fighting it. For children however, it might take some time for them to understand the way things work. Positive discipline parenting involves taking time to explain the law of cause and effect to your children and allowing them to face the natural consequences of their actions. Many times, we end up creating made-up consequences just to suit our own needs. Building on the example of the child who needs to be reminded to pack up his toys, a natural consequence of leaving his stuffed toy in the yard would be the toy getting beaten by rain. This is natural and hopefully, the child learns the right way to take care of his toys afterwards. This will be more beneficial in helping the child do better next time than seizing all his toys or sending him to bed immediately as punishment. The next time your child does not want to cooperate, hold on for some time and see if the natural consequences of said behavior motivate them to act better.

Positive discipline parenting is in sharp contrast with the traditional punitive discipline methods that a lot of people are familiar with. Apart from a high level of mutual respect, communication and encouragement, there are countless other ways by which this parenting method is more beneficial to children in the long term. Research has shown that traditional forms of discipline have temporary effects and can even result in more misbehavior from children.

Adler's Principle of Behavior Influence

Psychologist Alfred Adler believed that as humans, we all have two basic needs to feel significant and to belong. He provided us with some key principles which show us how to gain an understanding of human behavior and even possibly alter it. He was of the opinion that a child's personality is created in his or her first 5-6 years of life. Adler also believed that children form their personality as a direct response to the ongoing situations in their families. This is because children strive to please their parents and avoid feeling inferior. For instance, certain children may get their way through niceness which can become a sociable way of life. On the other hand, children who become uncaring and tough will also carry these traits into adulthood. In his theory concerning the psychology of child behavior, Adler provides insight on how children develop psychologically and what motivates their various actions.

According to him, children need to feel like they belong, and this is why they will engage in purposeful behavior with that goal in mind. Adler believed that all children are born with an inferiority complex and will spend their entire lives trying to make up for it. As parents or guardians, the task becomes motivating your child to be responsible for their own behavior and to teach him or her to be respectful of themselves and other people. If, for example, your child talks to you disrespectfully, laying the groundwork with him or her will help them to realize that consequences will be enforced. In turn, they learn how to take responsibility for their behaviors and will lean towards cooperative and helpful behaviors instead.

To encourage positive behavior in your child, the use of encouragement as well as taking note of and appreciating their contributions go a long way. Just a simple "thank you" and telling them how helpful they are being can be all the encouragement they need at a given time. For example, instead of praising your child for taking his or her plate to the sink, you can be encouraging by letting them know you appreciate the help. At the other end of the spectrum, if the child spills some food while carrying the plate and you fixate on that instead of acknowledging the attempt, they will feel discouraged. In turn, there will be a higher chance of them acting in ways that are less acceptable later on.

Adler On the Logic Behind Child Misbehavior

When children do not get all that they need to overcome this inferiority complex that they are born with, their next line of action is to misbehave. They do this in any of the four ways below:

1. Make demands and exhibit bad behavior to get attention.

2. Resist, cause conflict and argue to gain control or power.
3. Hurt their parents verbally, physically or through a proxy such as a sibling to get revenge.
4. Get depressed or apathetic to show inadequacy.

One important thing to note about the way children behave is that it is never random, and they are always particular about the things they want. To find the reason why your child is acting in a certain way, you need to first examine how you react to that behavior. It is common for caregivers and parents to react emotionally instead of trying to see things from the child's perspective. A child who does not want to get out of bed in the morning to leave for school may actually be trying to gain some power over himself or herself. It may be that this child lacks a sense of belonging or feels like all adults do is boss him or her around. For this reason, refusing to get out of bed may be their own way of grabbing control when possible.

Has your older child ever hit his or her younger sibling? In such a situation, it is likely that you will feel scared and worry whether your little one is in a safe environment. However, what could be happening is that the older child simply wants revenge. Having to hear about how adorable his or her younger sibling is and being ignored might be frustrating and so they decide to take matters into their own hands. Or maybe a child is constantly running about the house and slamming into things. To adults, this is simply wrong and should not be condoned but to a tender young mind, this is the best way to get needed attention. Because the child in question has received the attention they crave by doing this in the past, they see this action as a means of feeling significant.

Asides from every child's psychological goals of getting

control, revenge, attention or showing inadequacy, biological needs may also contribute to misbehavior. Hunger, sickness, tiredness, or physical discomfort should be checked first before examining the psychological reason for the misbehavior. In Adler's teachings, a lot of focus is placed on getting rid of insecurities, creating a connection between children, families, and social environments, and helping the children to find significance in ways that are socially acceptable. It is recommended that parents take the time to connect the dots and decide on a parenting method that will make it easier for your child to bond with you and find significance in your family.

Did you know that the amount of connection your child feels with you as well as their significance in the family goes a long way in determining the coping strategies they will make use of throughout their lives? The family setting is the first real social setting children are exposed to and they will definitely imbibe the things you say and do. Apart from providing guidance, parenting can also be viewed as a sort of mirrored living because you have very loyal spectators hanging on to your every word. In parenthood, everything begins with the parents and your children's personalities will be greatly influenced by you—how true is this? In the following chapter, we will discuss the significance of parental influence on a child's personality as well as how your own personality, as a parent, affects your child's overall development.

Chapter Summary

- Positive discipline teaches children to cultivate self-control while punishment deals with controlling a child.
- Mutual respect and regular communication are vital in disciplining children positively.
- All humans, including children, have two major needs of feeling like they belong and feeling significant as well.
- Children misbehave to either get attention, gain control, get revenge or show inadequacy.

In the next chapter you will learn about the role of your personality as a parent in your child's overall development.

3

EVERYTHING STARTS WITH YOU

"I'M WATCHING YOU." ALTHOUGH IT DEPENDS ON THE context in which they are used, these are words that many of us feel uncomfortable hearing. As soon as we hear it, we get extra conscious of our actions and get very worried whether we are doing the right things. In parenting, it is more or less like these words are unspoken by your children but are there all the same. This is because children closely follow each of their parents' actions and words and will reciprocate in one way or the other. Parental influence is one of the most important factors that contribute to personality development. For example, children who have parents with high self-esteem tend to have good self-esteem too. Parents who have recorded high academic success typically have children who will meet and also surpass their own achievements. Children raised in divorced families have a higher chance of being divorced too and children who have happily married parents will likely find happiness in their adult relationships.

To Alfred Adler, both father and mother influence a child's personality development, especially the mother during the first stages of life. How you behave with a child, how much you allow them to socialize, the kind of culture they are subjected to, your emotional make-up, all have a great influence on your child's mental growth. You're more or less a role model to them and extra care should be taken to ensure you do a good job. Each time you take a specific action, react to people or things in some way, or say something, your child is observing what you do. It is through this same channel that infants pick up language skills and learn how to talk eventually. For young children, they depend on observation to navigate through the details of interpersonal relationships. Even as teenagers, children still pay attention to your words and actions and will watch how you handle all areas of your own life closely. Being a parent and being a role model go hand in hand—whether you like it or not.

Parenting is a constant job and it's not something you can get away from when you feel like it. Parenting and child development are closely linked and for optimal development, there has to be proper parenting. The first 5 years of a child's life is when the foundation of his or her personality is laid. At every stage of personality development, the child has to experience and surmount some form of existential crises to form a personality that is well-rounded. Below are each of these stages and how they influence a child's personality-

Infancy: This is the stage during which the child is between 0 to 18 months old and is learning to trust or mistrust people. Their primary need at this point is nourishment and tender affection. Having an attentive parent or caregiver who fulfills their needs quickly will help them learn to be trustful, improve their confidence and motivate them to be happy toddlers. On the other hand, children this age will get anxious and become mistrusting when their needs are not met. At this point, parents or caregivers need to respond to them warmly and attend to their needs as quickly as possible.

Early childhood: When children are between 1 and a half to 3 years of age, they are in the second stage of emotional and social development. It is during this stage that they begin to explore independence in contrast with shame or doubt. By this time, their nervous and motor skills are significantly developed and so they want to explore their surroundings on their own. Children need to be watched and given needed guidance now. To boost their independence and confidence, they can be allowed to speak up in decisions concerning them. Not giving them the freedom to do what they want as much as is logical or hovering over them every time can lead to self-doubt and impair the child's confidence. By guiding toddlers as and when they require it, they have the opportunity to try guided exploration and also develop their own thoughts about things.

Middle childhood: This stage is marked by initiative in contrast to guilt and usually occurs between the ages of 3 to 5 years. Children learn how to function independently during this time, and they become more assertive. They will want to try new things and will also work on building relationships with other children and doing things together. These shared activities help your child to develop a sense of self-confidence and initiative. Asides from this, the child will be able to channel inner energy constructively and it will also give him or her a feeling of being happily occupied. Preventing your children from taking initiatives or criticizing their initiatives can impede their development and prevent them from completing this stage successfully. This, in turn, can leave the child feeling guilty.

Late childhood: This fourth stage of development is characterized by industry in contrast with inferiority. Between the ages of 5 and 12 years, children experience an increase in their strength and attention span. When this happens, they feel a need to learn new skills and will begin to compare themselves with other people to know where they stand. When they are able to complete a task successfully, they get very delighted and feel a sense of pride. If a child's competence is acknowledged, he or she will likely show more industriousness and work towards achieving set goals. On the other hand, if this budding trait is not encouraged, they may start developing self-doubt and inferiority complex which can hinder them from realizing their true abilities later on.

Adolescence: This stage is marked by identity or confusion and during this stage, teenagers are concerned with finding their fit within society and also discovering their personal identity. Between 12 to 18 years, they want more independence and will develop their own views about life. At this phase, children are trying to find their role within the family, the society, and in the professional area. To pass through this stage without issues, they need to be supported by their parents and their peers.

Did you know that the way you raise your children will tell on their cognitive, socio-cultural, physical, mental, and spiritual development? All of these are interrelated, and parents need to be actively present to make sure that the child's growing years run smoothly. Below are the 5 key areas of child development and how positive parenting affects each of them-

Cognitive: As parents, you have a huge influence on how developed your children's cognitive, problem-solving, and social skills will be. Proper parenting helps to improve these abilities and helps them grow to be better people. During their early years, children need a lot of interaction and stimulation. The way you handle situations, solve problems, manage your time, and discipline yourself are traits that they will likely pick up too.

Socio-cultural: There can be no doubt that children are keen observers, and they will pay attention to how you interact with your spouse and how arguments get settled. By doing this, they too learn how to behave with and around other people.

Physical: With the right guidance from their parents, children can learn about their health, exercise regularly and eat a diet that promotes proper physical development. If you are someone who cares about fitness and proper diet, there is a higher chance that your children will too.

Mental: Depending on the parenting style, children can learn to accept and overcome failures, understand discipline, and accept feedback. Parenting styles largely influence the way children respond to stimuli and is therefore a way of molding their minds.

Spiritual: Children learn ethical values, empathy, religion, discernment between right and wrong, and so on from their parents. By teaching them to believe in the greater good and be more accepting, we help them in developing a sense of purpose.

It can be quite overwhelming to realize just how much effect your words and actions have on your young one's life. However, keeping in mind that children learn from what goes on around them, particularly from their parents will help you remain in check. Here are some useful tips that you can use in parenting to make this journey even easier for you-

1. **Remain positive at all times.** It can be very easy for kids to sense negativity so you should try to keep that away as much as possible. Regardless of your child's age, talk to them about your problems and the ways you tackle them. You could also encourage them to partake in little household tasks with you. Times like this are an opportunity to teach them creativity and problem-solving with a positive attitude.

2. **Take care of yourself.** When was the last time you truly had a good night's rest? Is it a time long ago buried amidst other memories? If so, it might be taking its toll on you in relation to your parenting. When we are exhausted, it becomes much easier for us to lose our patience with our children in situations where they want to take their time or explore. Maria, mum to 2 1/2-year-old Rea says, "If I'm properly rested, I have no problem with letting Rea take all the time she wants brushing her teeth, as long as we don't have anywhere to rush off to. On the days I don't get adequate rest and feel aches all over though, my voice tends to be sharper and I'm usually more on edge." Many of us are no strangers to the problems of dealing with children, especially when we're not feeling so great ourselves. However, allowing ourselves to get even slightly aggressive towards them at that moment will only lead to more tantrums and power struggles. It comes down to taking a break when needed to get proper rest. Devoting all our time to attend to our children might not be the best idea after all.

3. **Be emotionally present.** Create an atmosphere of love and encouragement as much as you can

within your household. By letting your child know that you are always available to him or her and that they are loved, proper all-round development is guaranteed.

4. **Stop helping with things they can handle.** It is common for many parents to see their children trying to do something and before they know it, they're up on their feet doing it for them already. While this can be thought of as caring for the child in question, it can also be very detrimental to their development. Taking time to teach children how to do self-care goes a long way in building their confidence and self-esteem. For example, a child who keeps trying to put on socks on their own is showing that he or she is interested in dressing themselves. This would be a good time to show them the basics of getting dressed such as putting one leg at a time into their pants. Children have an amazing amount of untapped potential and so you should never think that they're too young to handle certain things. Do yourself a favor and give your child some basic dress-up training—you might be shocked to discover that they can handle everything from their underwear to socks and may only need your help with wearing a top. Sometimes, we think that kids will learn how to do certain things like this on their own eventually—however, early training and guidance will be more beneficial instead.

5. **Be affectionate towards everyone.** To children, swearing, constant fighting, loud quarrels, the use of harsh words and so on will be completely okay if that is the norm in the home. It is best for parents to pay close attention to their interactions,

especially in the presence of their children and their impressionable minds.

6. **Change your impression of mistakes.** For many of us while growing up, mistakes were bad things that were to be avoided at all costs. In that same vein, we have a tendency to pass this unhealthy notion to our kids. We need to teach our children that mistakes should be seen as opportunities to learn and not a sort of misdeed. Rather than trying to save them from making mistakes, we should use such opportunities to show them how to react to such situations. If a child spills a cup of water, for instance, it can be a chance to show him or her what to do in such a situation and invite them to help with mopping the area. The next time when something similar happens and you ask the child how to fix it, you'll be amazed at how much they will have learned.

7. **Keep the lines of communication open.** Sometimes, we assume we know our children's thoughts and think we're making the best choices on their behalf. However, it is best to talk to children and hear what they have to say before we draw any conclusions. In every conversation we have with our children, we should try to view things from their own perspective and allow them to express themselves. Effective communication will help you to know just what is going on in your child's mind.

8. **Be less controlling.** Most of the time, we tend to lecture our kids and dish out commands, corrections, and directions as parents. This might be causing more harm than good as children have a lower

chance of cooperating this way. "I noticed that giving Adrian firm directives and commands only made him even more unbending. He just wouldn't cooperate that way," Drew says. We need to remember that children are humans just like us— how much do you enjoy being talked at and told what to do in every situation? It's no surprise that kids who are raised this way are more likely to rebel or go against set rules which will only compound problems. By releasing our grip on the reins just a little, it will be easier for us to pay attention to the more important areas of parenting like proper teaching and guidance.

9. **Stick to a routine.** Setting routines for sleep, eating and play will help your children to start learning useful habits for the future. Going to bed on time, sleeping on time, turning off the tv during meals, and so on are good routines that children can pick up and learn to follow as well.

10. **Have discussions in advance about certain situations.** Letting kids know how different situations will be handled beforehand can help reduce the likelihood of misbehavior. For example, if a child suddenly stops putting his or her clothes in the dirty hamper as usual, you can tell them in advance that the clothes on the floor will be seen as trash and thrown away as appropriate. This helps the child to realize the consequence of dropping clothes on the floor and take needed steps to prevent it. Children can also be taught to interact with you respectfully without interruptions while on the phone by discussing the consequences of doing so in

advance. This could be you going outside or going into another room instead.

As parents, we have a great deal of work to do in order to ensure the proper development of our children in all areas of their lives.

You are your child's role model and the examples you lay down for them today will go a long way in shaping who they become tomorrow. In the next chapter, we'll see how we as parents can lead by example and help our children cultivate valuable social skills too by extension.

Chapter Summary

- Parents are role models to children and should be conscious of exhibiting healthy behaviors at all times.
- Each stage in a child's life is marked by different aspects of personality development.
- Your personality affects your child's cognitive, physical, socio-cultural, mental, and spiritual development.
- In order for children to develop optimally, we need to give them proper parenting.

In the next chapter you will learn how you can lead by example and help your wards to also cultivate valuable social skills by extension.

4

MODEL POSITIVE DISCIPLINE

"He's a chip off the old block." "She's just like her mother." "The apple doesn't fall too far from the tree." All these familiar sayings help to drive home the point that children will grow to be like their parents in one way or another. A lot of psychologists are of the opinion that more than 95% of a person's behavior is through imitation of people around them, particularly in the childhood and adolescent stages. This alone emphasizes the need for us to be good role models to our kids. They will learn from example the things that they might not grasp through repeated instructions. At birth, children have very limited knowledge about life and so they look up to their parents to teach them important life lessons and values. Parents can be seen as evolving and consistent role models as they regularly interact and spend time with their children. Children do not have a say in who their parents will be and you, as a parent, are a major influence on your child's behavior.

In parenting, children will do as you do and not only as you say—it's just the way they are. From very early ages, they begin to watch their parents and imitate the behaviors they see. To this end, if there's a particular behavior you wouldn't want your children picking up, you will likely have to get rid of it. The way you behave lets your child know the kind of behavior that is acceptable. Observing a behavior that is different from what you tell them will only confuse them or even make them resentful. This may also blur the boundaries and expectations you have for your child. We should try to prevent ourselves from doing anything we would not want our kids to see us involved in. Role modeling can serve as a very useful parenting tool and to be positive role models for our children, we need to apply adequate self-control and forethought. There's a lot of discussions on how children should be disciplined these days and not enough on how parents should discipline themselves too. It is very easy to make a list of the things we don't want our kids doing but we also need to make some effort to be practitioners of what we teach them. To be good parents and give our children adequate support as they grow, we need to be patient, calm and resilient.

Have you ever been advised to "parent by example"? If so, that is the best and simplest parenting advice anyone will ever give to you. However, as simple as it sounds, bad days come round for all of us and we end up engaging in arguments or saying things we will likely regret later on. Regardless of how beneficial this advice can be, the fact remains that nobody is perfect, and a day will come when we'll do or say things we'd prefer our children to not be aware of. What do we do next in such situations?

Well, the actions we take after missteps like this have as much significance as our initial actions. These important moments give us the chance to display valuable emotions such as empathy, forgiveness, and humility which we'd want our children to pick up as well. It can be very easy for us to tell our kids that we value morals like loyalty, forgiveness, honesty, and so on but if we don't practice them in our daily lives, there is no way our kids will learn them. For example, if you had an argument with your spouse and said some unkind things, a proper apology, and discussions to make amends will serve as a great example for your children. In a similar vein, being empathetic towards our children when they're upset or disciplining them lovingly and patiently teaches them to empathize with other people and also distinguish wrong from right without compromising the values you're trying to teach them. Let's say it's a sunny afternoon and you've been trying to get your child to stop screaming at the top of his lungs to no avail. In a sudden burst of frustration, you yell "stop screaming!" at him to drive home your point. Even if this turns out to be effective and the child goes quiet due to fear or some other reason, you have merely displayed the exact behavior that you're trying to discourage in him.

Role modeling can be useful in virtually all aspects of living from the way you handle your emotions, to your interactions with others, to how you take care of yourself, and so on. The best way to be positive role models for our kids is by showing them how to be the people we want them to be. Most of the important ways we can lead by example are through things we do on a daily basis—we only need to be more conscious of the fact that our children are learning as we do these things. For one, showing care and respect in your own behavior will help your children to choose relationships that are respectful and also work towards cultivating them as well. If you are in a disrespectful relationship, talking to the other party or seeking professional help are some positive ways of resolving the issue that you can model. Learning to stand up for yourself respectfully too will help children to learn vital skills and ways of relating with other people. If you're someone who makes education seem fun and interesting, there is a higher chance that your child will have a positive attitude towards school and learning. Reading about a new topic or even reading for pleasure is a great way to encourage children to pick up their books as well. Similarly, your use of technology will send your kids strong messages about how much importance it has in your family life. Needless to say, your child will automatically believe that your phone is your most prized possession if you're always walking around with it. While we cannot completely banish our mobile devices, discipline (which is the major theme of this book) will help us to devote our time to more important things. For example, being on social media for some time and then taking a walk with your family communicates to your child that it is just an option for relaxation and entertainment and not a do-or-die activity.

Qualities of A Positive Role Model

They are passionate and inspirational. Positive role models are passionate about their interests and can even infect other people with their passion. They have the ability to inspire and are dedicated to teaching, helping and empowering their children. To be positive role models, we need to always be ready to give back to the coming generation.

They are selfless and accepting of others. Accepting people who are different from us and being selfless is another quality positive role models have. Regardless of a person's circumstance or background, we should always be ready to render help to those in need. By ignoring social barriers and assisting those we can, we lay down an example of selflessness for our kids.

They are committed to their community. Instead of being focused on only themselves, good role models pay attention to other people as well. They are usually active participants in their communities and give their talents and time freely to the benefit of other people.

They are resilient. The ability to keep moving forward even in the presence of obstacles is a valuable trait commonly displayed by positive role models. By learning to overcome obstacles, we help our children develop their initiative and also prove to them that success can be achieved.

They have clear values. Every day is an opportunity for us as parents to live the values we teach to our children. Children have admiration for people whose actions are in alignment with their beliefs because it shows them how their own values and personalities are connected. It also shows them how they can find fulfilling roles as they grow older.

There are many ways by which parents can be positive role models for their children. Below are 16 of such ways which you too can make use of.

Spend enough time with them—As parents, it can be easy for us to get so preoccupied with work or our personal affairs that we don't realize we are spending too little time with our kids. While providing them with clothes and toys are important too, this is simply not enough. By spending quality time with our children, we build a strong foundation within the relationship. This also helps to fill in the gap between our generation and their younger one which makes it possible for us to identify and also understand them better.

Don't hide details about your life from them—Your child needs to know who you truly are and the things you are capable of. Nobody is perfect and we all falter or make mistakes. Talking to children about mistakes you have made will help them to learn from your own experiences. Pretending to be who you're not by presenting an unrealistically positive image of yourself will not be beneficial to you or your children in the long run. Bear in mind that the way you react towards the drawbacks or failures that come your way will help your child to develop a strong character.

Be ready to listen at all times—A lot of children are very outspoken around their parents and they'll want to share their thoughts with you on a daily basis. Sticking to the wrongful notion that children should only be seen and not heard can be very detrimental to child development. No matter how immature or silly the things they say might seem to you, it's best to lend a listening ear and show that you're interested. Listening to your children is very vital in knowing and understanding the events going on in their lives. Being disinterested in what your kids have to tell you will make it much harder for you to know their true thoughts and intentions. By being good listeners to our children's concerns, stories, fears, or issues, we get to know them better and also reassure them that they are free to share anything with us.

Start early—You might think that it's too early to start setting good examples for your kids or start inculcating positive values in them. However, little children have very fertile minds and even if their communication skills are still budding, their minds and feelings make it possible for them to pick up new things. If you want your kids to learn important virtues, start teaching them now. By taking little steps in that direction starting now, it will be easier for them to model such behaviors as they grow rather than you having to expend huge effort in teaching them later on.

Be respectful towards yourself and other people —How do you speak to and about your family members, friends, neighbors, and yourself? Do you show respect for them? Are you kind with your words? By watching the example you set, children learn the amount of value to give to institutions and people around them. How often do you say the words "please," "sorry," "excuse me," "thank you," and so on? Your use or lack of use of these will set the tone for how your kids will interact with people when they grow older too. Children can also learn to appreciate their self-worth from the way we treat ourselves—when we respect ourselves, they will definitely watch and follow our lead.

Radiate positivity at all times—Although it might be difficult to do this at all times, positivity is one of the best things parents can express towards their children. If we're able to remain positive during times that are particularly testing or tough, our children will also adopt the same positive mindset. Learn to focus on the positive aspects of every situation as kids can begin to develop a negative outlook right from within the home. Always see the cup as half-full and not half-empty. The next time you make a mistake, carefully consider your reactions to it. For example, if you burnt dinner for the evening, have a hearty laugh about it and appreciate the chance to order food. Simple mistakes like these are usually the best opportunities for us as parents to model good behavior.

Manage your anger—Maybe you've seen your little one

throw fits or get very agitated frequently when he or she is denied certain things. The question to ask ourselves at this point is "How do I respond to unfavorable circumstances too? Do I lash out at anybody?" The ways by which we respond to hurt feelings, anger and stress serve as models for our children to follow. Our society can be so stressful, fast-paced and demanding sometimes that we tend to naturally react with anger. However, we should try not to let this affect us adversely as much as possible. When we face challenges, it is best to stay calm, breathe deeply and talk through it. We could even discuss the trigger with our children and how we handled it if it is appropriate. By doing so, our children learn to calm down and consider their reactions carefully when next something triggers them.

Be encouraging—Children are extremely sensitive and as they grow, they get even more sensitive about their parents' words than anyone else. It is not uncommon to see that a lot of children are very particular about the encouragement and approval of their parents. Encouraging our children consistently helps to improve their self-confidence and also builds their character. Each child is unique, and they all have distinct characteristics and qualities. Parents need to appreciate their children's qualities and also encourage their endeavors and efforts. Try not to nag your children or set unreasonably high expectations that may be beyond their capacity for them. We should be good encouragers and patient advisors for our children on all issues of life. Even when they make mistakes or fail, loving words of encouragement go a long way in developing their character positively.

Use the right tone with your children—Aside from our words, children also pay a great deal of attention to our tone as it can express a whole lot. When trying to make a point, never shout or yell at your kids as this will only hurt them and scare them off—remember that children need to always be confident that they can turn to you. It is best to give clear and firm instructions to children and then leave the rest to their discretion. Let your child know what you want of them by giving simple instructions rather than using a confusing tone that can leave room for ambiguity.

Model proper etiquette—Basic things like hand washing, cleaning up, brushing the teeth, setting and clearing up the table are positive actions that you can demonstrate for your children. Endeavor to carry out these actions in front of your children and emphasize them as you do so. For example, if you have taught your children to wash their hands before eating, asking them a question like "what do we do before we eat?" at each mealtime will help them to remember this and imbibe it properly.

Set goals—Some important aspects of child upbringing include setting goals, implementing them, and then achieving them. These three vital aspects can be applied to all spheres of a child's life be it behavior or academics to produce excellent results in all areas of life. Parents should encourage their children to share their goals, aspirations, and dreams with them so as to enable them to work hand in hand to achieve them.

Volunteer in your community—By doing this, we show our kids that we have concern for the world they live in and they also learn to care too. Donating food or supplies, partaking in cleaning up the community or volunteering in schools are ways we show our kids that what happens outside your home is just as important as what happens within. Selfless acts such as these help children to realize that giving back goes a long way in making the world a better place.

Watch your usage of alcohol and drugs—In our society today, many children have fallen victim to the misuse of drugs and alcohol due to peer pressure and the influence of friends. However, parents also have a major influence in the chances of this happening. Are you a regular heavy drinker? Do you misuse drugs as you please? If you answered "yes" to any of these questions, realize that your actions will affect your child's behaviors and attitudes too. Drinking moderately and occasionally rather than heavily on a daily basis will send our children good messages about the habits they should cultivate.

Work hard—Every child needs to cultivate a good work ethic whether in school, on the sports team, at a job, or anywhere else. Modeling this behavior at home is a fantastic way to instill this vital life skill in them. Regardless of whether you work from home or go to work on a daily basis, make sure that your children see you working. A simple but effective way to instill a proper work ethic in children is by doing household chores with them as a family.

Teach them new skills—The best way to teach children new things is by showing them how to do it and then allowing them to practice on their own. Whether you're trying to help your child learn to tie their shoes or make their bed, showing them instead of telling will help them to learn new skills.

Try not to overdo it—Although done with pure intentions, parents can go overboard in trying to be good role models for their kids sometimes. Praising, pampering, or showering our kids with so much love may actually end up making them uncomfortable. Children will see beneath the insincerity eventually, so we need to ensure that all our actions and words are genuine.

Importance of Role Models for Children

Attitude and personality—As children pay close attention to the actions of their parents and follow them, they also adapt their attitude and personality traits. The way we react to certain circumstances or situations will often determine what action our children will take. By observing the attitude and personality of their parents, kids learn to dislike or like certain things as the case may be.

Social relationships—Children view social relationships based on how important these relationships are to their role models. Your outlook on public or family relationships will be reflected in the way your children express their feelings. Therefore, if you place little importance or have little regard for family life, your children likely will too.

Life perception—We know that children observe things keenly and as soon as they pick up something, there is a very high chance that it will remain with them throughout their lives. They have a tendency to view life from the perspective of people who are close to them, especially their parents. Their role models are their standards of measurement and so they will see themselves based on their similarity to you or how you look at them.

Ambitions and aspirations—Are you ambitious? Are there certain things you go after in life or are you simply okay with anything that comes your way? Your attitudes toward this aspect of your life will also influence your children—positively or negatively. Their efforts and determination towards fulfilling their dreams depends on the example that you have laid down for them.

The question we need to ask ourselves now is "Am I a good role model for my child/children?" If you haven't been, it is never too late to start. Give yourself the challenge of identifying positive things that you can model for your children like consideration, generosity, kindness, self-discipline, compassion, self-respect, diligence, and so on. Regular exercise to improve your mental and physical health, reading to expand your mind, spending time with family and friends are also other positive traits that can be role modeled for your children. Remember that kids see beneath the façade and being hypocritical will disillusion them and cause them to look for other people to follow. Let your words align with your actions and your children will continue to have admiration for and confidence in you.

At the same time, children may learn misbehaviors from other people no matter how hard we try to model good morals. He or she may find it hard to share with others, hide the truth about certain things and so on. Regardless of the behavior displayed, be sure to use the situation as an opportunity to learn rather than chastise them. Children become what they see and believe so it is important for us to build a good legacy for them to inherit. Starting right from now, make the conscious decision to be a parent that models good traits that can be believed in and built upon.

The environment in which a child grows is very crucial to their success and wellbeing. The home environment is one that plays a significant role in proper child development and should be given adequate attention. In the following chapter, we will take a look at the role of the home environment in child development and how we can create one that is positive and nurturing for them.

Chapter Summary

- Children pay attention to the things we do and not just what we say.
- Mistakes along the way give us the opportunity to show emotions like humility, forgiveness, and empathy.
- Children will admire and be more confident in you when your words align with our actions.
- When your child misbehaves, use that opportunity to teach them and not chastise them.

In the next chapter you will learn the role of the home environment in child development and how to create a positive and nurturing home environment for your child.

5

CREATE THE ENVIRONMENT FOR SUCCESS

The home environment little children grow up in goes a long way in determining their chances for proper development and survival. It influences all aspects of their development including their thoughts, behaviors, growth, and emotions. Environments that are nurturing promote good health outcomes and reduce the occurrence of developmental challenges. In order for children to explore, learn and grow, they need a home that is safe and healthy. Growing up in a stressful home environment can adversely affect their emotional, social, and intellectual growth. Apart from impaired development, research shows that an unhealthy home environment in the first years of life can cause behavioral issues, poor language skills, depression, and so on. There are also brain imaging studies that suggest that the brains of children who grow up in stressful or disadvantaged environments can develop differently. As parents, we have the huge responsibility of providing the best environment for our children as their behavior, learning, and personality are on the line. Your home environment should be filled with positivity, happiness, and love. When we give children the solid foundation they need during their early stages, they can handle things that come their way better.

Children are like little seedlings and when we provide them with good soil, sufficient sunlight and water, they will grow deep and sturdy. The home environment needs to be one that gives them proper nourishment and helps them to thrive. It includes everything you do with your family and the places you give your children access to that influence their learning and development. It also covers daily experiences that help them to make their own sense of the world and the chances they get to play and engage with objects and books. Providing a good home environment for children encourages them to be self-confident, curious, and to develop good attitudes towards learning. In order for them to reach their full potential, they need time in an environment that is responsive and caring and caters to their needs. During their early years, children need adequate interaction with adults who sing to them, talk to them, and exchange eye contact. At this stage, they are naturally curious and should be provided with various natural materials and everyday objects to investigate.

These days, it can be even more challenging to provide nurturing environments for our kids than ever before. This is because many children do not have yards, neighborhoods, or spaces where they can safely explore for hours. Even if these are present, there are already so many planned activities that take up all their time. Regardless of the reason behind it, the fact remains that an increasing number of children spend their time within buildings than they do outside. What this implies is that the home environment is the major area that your children will mostly interact with—therefore, it needs to provide them with maximum benefits.

The same way kids have little control over their environment is the same way we as parents have little say in what goes on in the world around us. No single person can put a stop to all the violence, injustice, crime, and hunger that abounds in our environment and these dangers will remain each day we step out. Although we can't end all the world problems, what we can do is to create an environment that protects the potential of our kids and helps it to grow properly. A lot of parents already feel too occupied trying to make a living to ensure their children are in safe spaces. We may feel like we don't have the energy or time to provide a better environment for our kids, but it is possible. Stella says, "I had to work two jobs when I had Abel. I was almost always pressed for time and my priority was making sure I provided him with his basic needs. However, I realized that asides from the material aspects, the environment I raised him in also mattered. I took out time to create a nurturing home environment for him and it's done us a whole lot of good." Nurturing environments help our kids to learn how to process and express their emotions as is age appropriate. It also promotes positive interactions with their peers and helps them to deal with stressful situations much better. While it may sound like a lot of work, the steps we take and efforts we put in now to provide a positive environment for our kids will prove to be useful to them and us, their parents, as well. For one, a more nurturing environment will allow us to spend more enjoyable time with our kids—how so? We all know how tiring and time-consuming it can be to struggle with our children's behaviors when their needs are unmet. However, placing them in an environment that nurtures them helps them to be even more delightful to be with as time goes on. The changes we have to make now will definitely be worth it eventually. If you're holding back from putting up that hammock because you can't spare a few hours, imagine the countless hours of cuddling, storytelling, comfort, and joy that you will get in return. Depending on what your family's interests and capacities are, there is a wide range of changes you can make as even the smallest ones can make huge differences in the lives of our children.

Providing our children with a nurturing space where they can thrive involves attending to their physical needs such as shelter and food and creating sensory-rich and warm environments where all aspects of their needs are acknowledged and met. In the last chapter, we emphasized that the experiences children have in their environment as they grow is what they will absorb and copy. This remains very true, and your child's potential will either be nurtured or limited by the environment you expose them to. To ensure proper growth, we need to create an environment that provides our children with the security and opportunity they need to make discoveries about themselves and their immediate world.

The way children recognize and understand their emotions is also significantly affected by their home environment. For example, children who grow up in homes with little expressivity can suffer from slow emotional development. On the other hand, children who are raised in home environments that are overly expressive such as abusive ones are better at recognizing vocal and facial anger cues than at identifying other emotions. A positive home environment gives young children the consistency they need to develop strongly during their childhood. The immediate environment they are exposed to helps in shaping their worldview, stability, and self-worth significantly. Sunday visits to the park, sharing meals together, and so on are some good opportunities for families to cultivate social relationships and encourage a sense of belonging among their children. Routines are also beneficial in helping children deal with stress like divorce or parental separation.

There are so many seemingly insignificant items and ways we can use to create an atmosphere that is loving and encouraging. In a home environment that is nurturing, more time should be spent together around the table than in front of the television. "Our family table is where we all come to get nurtured and nourished. We play games together, work on projects, have fun tea parties and so on. The valuable family time we all enjoy gathered around that table is much better than sitting in front of a screen," Marie says. Do you have a fireplace in your home? Coming together around a fire has always symbolized emotional and physical warmth and is an activity children greatly enjoy. Even in the absence of a fireplace, an act as little as lighting a candle at dinner can create that same warm feeling. One thing about young children is that they enjoy being inside or around water and simply filling a tub with water and empty containers will leave them content for hours. Each time we put our children in a bathtub or take them to a pool, lake, and so on, we are providing them with a nurturing environment. Gardening is another wonderful way to bond with children and help them feel a connection with nature and the earth. Kids enjoy digging in the dirt, planting seeds, and watching them grow just like anyone else. Even if we don't know a lot about gardening or have a garden space in our home, it is still possible for us to give our children that nurturing environment. Putting a seed in a jar of soil, planting a tree on their birthday, and recording the daily growth of flowers are some easy ways this can be done. Giving kids the opportunity to connect with living and growing things is a significant way to provide them with a nurturing environment.

As everyone has their own daily activities to attend to, it is vital that families have spaces where they can go to together. It could be a local library, your family place of worship, a shared community activity and so on. Apart from the positive environment this provides for our children, it can also be a great way for us, as parents to get rid of stress and enjoy some quality family time.

Maintaining a positive environment within the home is no child's play—a lot of hard work, concentration and persistence are key ingredients for doing so and it can be a lot to handle sometimes. However, if we start taking steps right from now to set and achieve set goals and guidelines, there is a higher chance of creating a pleasant home environment. Providing positive and loving discipline for our children right from a tender age will greatly reduce the chances of problems with their learning and development later on. There are some practices and rules which parents need to implement right from now as holding out till later can make it difficult for children to change their habits. In creating the right environment for our children, all members of the family have a vital role to play in ensuring that the environment is enabling and friendly. Family members should always be ready to listen to and show respect for one another as this helps in maintaining a home environment that is free from confusions.

One of the most significant things we can do as parents is encourage our kids as this goes a long way in helping them with their emotional development. It helps them to believe in their personal satisfaction, build self-esteem and feel secure within themselves. Their budding confidence is greatly increased when we pay them due attention and encourage them positively. We need to note that there is a significant difference between encouraging kids and praising them.

While praise focuses on the doer of an act or the end product, encouragement pays more attention to the deed that is done. An example of praise may sound like "You're such a good boy/girl" or "You got an A on the science test!" while encouragement is more like "Thank you for setting the table," "You worked really hard to get this grade on your test" or "I appreciate your help packing lunches." By encouraging children, more attention is given to what they actually did which can inspire them to repeat the action. Positive encouragement places more emphasis on the efforts our children make and how they can do even better in future.

The home environment is also important in setting the pace for a young child's learning as the right learning environment is established at home. For instance, young children should have the opportunity to do their homework in an area that is well-lit and devoid of distractions. They should be provided with pencils, paper, crayons, and other materials which will help them complete the task easily. Preparing such materials beforehand will help to save precious time and also ensure that children remain focused from start to finish. Setting up a prepared environment for young children is of maximum importance and in the next section, we'll take a look at Maria Montessori's thoughts on the significance of such for young children.

Maria Montessori On the Importance of a Prepared Environment for Children

Maria Montessori was an Italian educator among other things, who believed in the need for children to grow in what she referred to as a "prepared environment." She saw this kind of environment as one which is structured in a way that promotes complete exploration and independent learning by children. This kind of environment is one that allows for a high level of movement by children along with various activities for them. According to her, the primary purpose of the prepared environment is to render the growing child as independent of the adult as much as possible. Dr. Montessori believed that the period from birth till age six was the most important in a person's life and not adulthood as they are the formative years. It is during these early years that children need a prepared environment that gives them the freedom to build up their unique potentials with the aid of appropriate sensorial items. These sensorial materials help them to expand, classify, and express their sensory experiences as they take place. They play a huge role in the overall development of children including how they process weight, pitch, temperature and how they use language to describe these qualities.

Each kind of sensorial material that can be found in a prepared environment has a significant importance in improving the visual, tactile, olfactory/gustatory, and auditory abilities of young children.

Visual—Knobbed cylinders or cylinder blocks prepare children for math in the future as they build up the child's ability to differentiate size visually. Trinomial and binomial cubes help children to better appreciate three-dimensional beauty and prepares them indirectly for certain mathematical concepts.

Tactile—Thermic bottles and fabrics build up children's tactile senses as they feel different degrees of texture, softness, roughness, and temperature as they touch them. Geometric solids sharpen the way children visually perceive solid figures and boost their muscular-tactile sense.

Olfactory/Gustatory—Tasting and smelling bottles allow children to distinguish one smell or taste from the other and apply the knowledge to other tastes or smells in their environment.

Auditory—Bells and sound cylinders help young children to learn how to identify pitch and volume and increase their sensitivity to environmental sounds.

The prepared environment is ideal for children as they need to gather basic knowledge, experiment, and explore through direct experience. Childhood is that important time in a person's lives when they gain firsthand information about the abrasion of concrete on a bare knee, stink of rotting fruit, gravity's constant pull, and many other interesting aspects of the physical world. Environments that are play-based greatly encourage emotional and social development which enables young children to cultivate effective communication skills, proper problem-solving skills, and excellent academic skills. There is a need for a lot of stimulation at this point and if children are denied this, their mental growth will stagnate.

Components of A Prepared Environment

Structure and Order—A prepared environment should reflect the real world's structure and order. This enables the children to internalize the way their surroundings are arranged and start making sense of the world around them.

Nature and Reality—Nature should be used as a source of inspiration for children, and they should be allowed to interact with it regularly. Child-size and real natural learning materials made of bamboo, wood, etc. should be given to them so they can assess the materials without needing any help or getting frustrated.

Freedom—Freedom of choice can be achieved by allowing children freedom to interact, move, and explore on their own. Keeping a close watch on them and giving corrections as needed helps to improve their growing cognitive skills.

Social environment—A prepared environment encourages children to interact, thereby supporting their social development. Young children become more socially aware by developing empathy for other people and compassion.

Beauty—The atmosphere in a prepared environment is one that evokes harmony, peace, and tranquility. It is properly maintained, uncluttered, and inviting for children to learn.

Intellectual environment—A prepared environment nurtures a child's intellect as well as his or her complete personality.

How Can I Create the Right Environment for My Child?

With proper planning, we can create areas that encourage the engagement, development, and general wellbeing of our children. The environment we provide for them needs to be safe, enhance their learning, support positive relationships, and should be organized in a way that each of their needs can be catered to.

When creating an environment for our children, the first thing we need to think about is their safety and health within that environment. Designing safe spaces for them allows them to explore with freedom—this strengthens their sense of self and also supports us as parents. Rather than having to spend time constantly monitoring them to keep them safe, there are more chances for us to interact with them and respond to their needs. There are lesser chances of children getting hurt or contracting illness in an environment that is safe and healthy.

Responsive and respectful relationships are crucial to a young child's growth and development. For this reason, a positive environment should be one that promotes these. There should be room for meaningful interactions to take place between you and your child. You can do this by including areas like benches, floor cushions, and so on where you both can comfortably sit. Places like rocking chairs and couches where you can snuggle with your child to read together, offer them comfort, or have quiet interactions with each other should also be provided.

Your child's environment needs to be supportive of their development and so it should allow them to move around safely and freely. Ensure that the floors of the area are not slippery or littered and that there is a safe place for your child to land if he or she falls. At all levels of their development, children need safe areas that allow them to explore movement. For this reason, it is best to avoid putting them in restrictive devices that hinder their natural movement like highchairs or swings. Furniture should be arranged in ways that allow for easy passage so children can find their way around the room easily. To make it easier to watch over your child at all times, low dividers, shelves, and pieces of furniture that you can see over easily should be used in all areas of the room. Activities and toys can be arranged in baskets or trays on the low furniture to allow children to find the toy or activity of their choice without needing help from an adult. Child-friendly equipment and furniture that they can pull up, crawl through and so on should also be provided for them.

Rotating materials gives your child a balance of new and familiar materials which provides them with challenges that are appropriate for his or her age and also keeps them interested. We need to be careful not to offer too many materials at once as children can get overwhelmed when a room is cluttered.

As children grow, the environment needs to be adapted to suit their developmental needs and changes. Younger children need enough freedom to move around but as soon as they become mobile, their environmental needs will change as well. From time to time, it is important for parents to evaluate their children's environment and make needed changes to accommodate their needs and growing skills. This is an ongoing process that if done properly, will support continual learning and exploration and also enhance the quality of your children's space. Bear in mind that young children live in a world dominated by adults and so everything around is much bigger than their bodies. This can make it difficult for them to gain access to things they need or find interesting and even restrict their movement. Therefore, it is best to make use of child-sized tools and furniture in your home which will make them more successful in their activities and also make them happier.

Although it would be great for each household to replicate the full Montessori setup in their home environment, the fact remains that not all families have the finances or space to do so. However, there are still countless ways we can modify our current environment to cater to our children's needs for independence. When setting up our home environment, we need to see the room just as they do and give a limited number of choices of books or activities to avoid cluttering. Below are some easy ways to create a living room, entryway, bathroom, kitchen, and bedroom that allows children to move, explore and learn in safety.

Living Room

Simplify—Most of the toys we leave laying around for our children are those that they might not even use regularly. Is there a toy your child has not touched in up to one week? If so, you might need to switch it out. To create a nurturing environment and promote concentration, children should have a limited number of options available. The less toys we give to them, the lesser their chances of getting distracted. You can leave out a few of their favorite toys to play with and rotate them regularly when your child hasn't played with a particular toy for a while. Apart from helping to create an environment that is less cluttered, this also helps us to know the toys our children prefer.

Make sure all items are within reach—Your child is definitely much shorter than you and it can be quite frustrating for them to keep struggling to reach for things. Everything your child could need should be easily accessible and close to the ground. Consider the use of low shelves which they can easily reach items on and child-sized furniture. The use of low shelves helps to improve their sense of independence as they can reach for items on their own when they need to.

Add books and a resting place for them—To encourage a reading culture in your child, you can also include books in their play area. This makes it easy for both of you to enjoy some reading sessions from time to time. Get a child-sized bookshelf, add a number of books to it and switch them out as often as needed. Pillows or blankets too can also be added as they can be beneficial in helping your child relax and providing a soft landing spot for them.

Introduce some order—-Every toy or material your child plays with should have its designated home, be it on a shelf or in a specific basket. Children need a certain amount of order because it is familiar and therefore comforting. It's very easy for toys to end up everywhere when there's no designated place for them to be. With proper order, we promote our children's need for routine and repetition. When they know where each item goes, it becomes easy for them to locate it and also put it away all by themselves.

Add nature to the mix—Studies have shown that the presence of natural light can be beneficial in calming the mind and body. For this reason, it is advised that your child's spot in the living room should enjoy plenty of natural light. You could consider setting it up close to a window or any other area that receives enough sunlight. Flowers and plants are also other natural items that you can include to make your child's play area even more soothing.

Provide a workspace for them—Including a space for your child to work will help him or her to explore their creativity and also concentrate better. Having a child-sized armchair and table somewhere in your living room where they can spend time on their own every day will give them a sense of purpose. "I realized that Cole had a number of seats and tables that were simply laying in storage. Since I crafted out a spot for his seat and chalk table, he spends hours there drawing or putting his little fingers to work in some way," Sarah says. Children need to be given time and the right opportunities to explore their creative abilities and a workspace of their own is a great way to encourage this.

Entryway

Use low coat hooks—When children are given the task of preparing to leave their home, it helps them to pick up a lot of valuable life skills. This includes practical skills like independently selecting a coat or a jacket that is suitable for the weather. When children don't have to wait for an adult to get these items for them, they are encouraged to practice dressing themselves up as much as possible.

Have a drawer or container for keeping seasonal items—Seasonal items like sunglasses, umbrellas and so on should be stored in a designated place. This gives your child the opportunity to learn about different weathers as well as the items they need for each one. Even better, doing this reduces the chances of a power struggle when your little one wants to wear winter boots in the middle of summer.

Hang their art at their eye level—By giving their artwork visibility and placing it at their eye level, we personalize the space and communicate to our children that their work matters too. Washing tape or an acrylic frame can be used to display their art to allow for easy rotation.

Create a place for them to sit and an area for their shoes and boots—A low stool, bench, child-sized chair, or any other comfortable place where your child can sit to practice wearing their shoes on their own will be beneficial. A soft rug or the staircase's bottom step can also do the trick if you have limited space in your home. Providing a rack, basket or tray for them to keep their shoes will also reinforce routines and maintain order. To help them practice decision-making, offer them limited choices as this will be less overwhelming for them.

Consider fitting a mirror on the wall—In order for your child to develop a good sense of identity and self as they leave the house, a mirror at their level will be very useful. This allows them to see their outlook when they're fully dressed to leave home and also provides them with a practical life skill of cleaning the mirror.

Bathroom

Having a child-friendly bathroom goes a long way in helping children to master practical self-care skills such as brushing their teeth, washing their hands, toileting, and washing their body and hair.

Provide a step stool—A child-sized step stool makes it easier for children to reach the sink as well as any other supplies that are on the counter. This stool can also be used to reach up to the light switch and turn the light on and off which can be an exciting activity for young children.

Store needed items under the sink—A basket or drawer for storing towels and washcloths placed under the bathroom sink allows children to gather needed supplies for bath time or face washing. They can even be included in the routine of laundering, folding, and storing these items to give a sense of ownership and pride in their routine.

Have child-sized bathroom accessories—To make the hand washing routine easy for children, you can get an easy-to-use soap dispenser or simply divide a bar of soap into two. You could also consider a foam dispenser as they enjoy a fun sensory experience with them. Small hand towels or washcloths that they can easily make use of in wiping splashes and drying hands should also be provided.

Store items for brushing within reach—Your child's toothbrush and toothpaste should be kept in a drawer or on a counter they can reach on their own. You could also provide them with a cup for a drink of water before bed or rinsing their mouth. If you regularly have to struggle with your child to brush their teeth, having two different flavors of toothpaste for them to choose from can be useful as children find choices empowering.

Mount a low hook—Fixing a low hook in your bathroom will help your child to know where their towel should be hung after each bath.

Use toddler-sized bottles—Travel-size body wash and shampoo bottles are best for little children as they find it easier to handle them without exhausting the whole supply. Fill these up with only the needed amount for one wash at a time.

Reduce the number of toys—Although bath toys can help to make the bathing activity even more fun for kids, giving them too many at once will only distract them. Limit the number of toys they have access to at once and rotate them as needed to maintain your child's interest.

Have a box of tissues handy—To help with blowing their nose and so on, there should be a box of tissues within your child's reach. To reduce the chances of him or her getting distracted and using the entire box at once, a small basket in which you can put a few folded tissues can be beneficial.

Consider using routine cards—The use of these can help children to initiate tasks such as going to the bathroom or brushing their teeth on their own. Routine cards also help them to stay on track as they transition from one routine to the other.

Get a potty seat or chair—To encourage toileting independence, a potty chair or seat for the toilet along with a step stool is recommended. Place toilet paper close by and slowly show your child how to use it so that he or she can follow your movements.

Kitchen

Help your child reach the counter height—To make your kitchen more child-friendly, the first item you need is a raised platform. You can try getting one that can easily be converted into a table or a chair made out of sturdy wood. This helps children to satisfy their curiosity and see just what is happening on the counter. When your child is on the same level as you are, they can then help with and partake in different kinds of kitchen activities with you. These include watching the cooking process, watching dishes, setting the table, washing fruits, and so on.

Provide needed cleaning materials—We need to encourage our children to be more aware of their environment and that includes cleaning the table, sweeping, wiping spillages, and so on. As there is always something to be taken care of in the kitchen, it is a great place for them to start learning how to do this. A piece of cloth, a brush, and a child-sized dustpan are necessary tools your child needs to do this.

Allow them easy access to various items—A bottom drawer, low shelf or small cupboard your child can easily reach should be used for storing the utensils, plates and instruments he or she can use. This also makes it possible for them to help out with setting up the table. A low shelf's top surface can be used in keeping a water dispenser and healthy snacks your child can help himself or herself to as needed.

Make use of real glasses and cutlery—As children grow, we can start to replace their plastic plates, forks, and cups with real child-sized versions. Even though the chances of breaking something is increased, this helps them to start understanding the concept of responsibility. For younger children, wooden knives and steel cups can be used until they are a bit older to handle the real items.

Bedroom

Keep everything within their reach—Although it can be tempting to build your child's room with a particular design in mind, the decor you choose should take his or her actual height into consideration. You can try laying on the floor or sitting on the ground to have an idea of what your child is able to see and access.

Choose the right kind of bed—A floor bed is the popular choice amongst parents who want to make their children's bedroom more child-friendly. Starting from age 2 and above, this can be introduced to your child. Floor beds put children in charge of their independence and mobility as they can get into and out of their beds as needed without needing an adult to assist them. The freedom of movement that comes with this type of bed instills the freedom of thought in children as they naturally move towards the item of their choice when they wake up.

Carefully select the items they can reach—The objects and activities children come in contact with each day should be in alignment with their developmental needs. The items around them when they wake up need to be a limited number but should also be inspiring at the same time. Selecting entertaining items for them this way helps them cultivate good concentration skills and also embrace their interest for the day. Apart from that, placing everything where they can reach them with ease means that you no longer have to suggest or guess about activities.

Set up stations where they can get ready—Your child's bedroom needs to feel like a sanctuary for them and so you should consider some practical ways through which they can make use of it. An area that is exactly their height with a hairbrush, mirror, or any other item they need in getting ready could be set up. Instead of tall dresser drawers, you could also use a lower rail in their cupboard or closet to store shirts and socks. Chairs and a table for carrying out projects or a reading nook could also be included.

Use age-appropriate ambiance and wall decor—When setting up a child's room, we need to view things from their perspective and not from that of an adult. Remember that the bedroom is your child's space and you're only setting it up to help them be more successful. Consider the art they'll like and place it at a level where they can actually see them. A natural muted tone or white paint helps in promoting a sense of calm, draws attention to wall art and also supports a relaxed environment.

Tips for Creating A More Child-Friendly Environment

- Find child-sized furniture your child can manage without needing any assistance.
- Carefully set out inviting age-appropriate activities on shelves for them.
- View things from their perspective and try to see the space through your child's eyes.
- Set up a little nest or bed in a quiet area for nap time.
- Keep in mind that less is more and display only activities your child is currently trying to master.
- Vacuum your home thoroughly and at short intervals if you have pets.
- Fill up an old tin with markers, crayons, and colored pencils for your child to play with.
- Create a space for every item and ensure that every item is always kept in their place.
- Beautify the area with plants and art your child can enjoy at their height.
- Store away extra items and activities carefully and rotate them regularly.

The way your home operates will largely determine your child's morals and overall development. We need to devote time in creating a positive environment that nurtures and protects their potential to ensure success. Even though we have our daily tasks and schedules, it is still possible to create a child-friendly environment with a couple of modifications and adjustments. Providing a positive and nurturing home environment will definitely require some effort on our parts but if we strive to do so now, our children and our home will be the better for it.

There can be no doubt that children need limits—this helps them to know just how far they are allowed to go without jeopardizing their physical, emotional, and general wellbeing. In the next chapter, we will take a look at the importance of setting limits for our children and how we, as parents can learn to draw the line kindly, but effectively.

Chapter Summary

- The home environment affects all aspects of a child's development from their thoughts to their emotions.
- Our duty as parents is to create a home environment that nurtures and preserves our children's potentials.
- We need to implement certain rules and practices starting from now to make it easier for our children to imbibe them.
- A prepared environment allows children to explore and learn on their own and should be provided in all areas of the home as much as possible.

In the next chapter you will learn the importance of setting limits for children and how to set limits that are kind, but also effective.

6

SETTING KIND AND FIRM LIMITS

KNOWING WHEN TO SAY NO TO OUR KIDS CAN RIGHTFULLY be seen as one of the hardest parts of parenting. As soon as children learn how to speak and understand languages, it might seem like we constantly have to use the words "stop", "don't do that", "no" or some other words along those lines. Setting limits can be even harder for single parents as all the discipline is up to them. Although it can be tiring to have to do this at times, and we might even feel like we're being the bad guys in the situation, the fact remains that boundaries are a vital part of parenting and setting them is one of the best things we can do for our children. Setting limits with them implies creating a guideline for behavior and helps them to know the kind of behaviors you discourage.

Rules are a natural aspect of life and with them, children learn how to deal with different situations and also know what we expect of them in the home, when they're with friends, and even in school. It can be tempting to hold back from setting rules for our children for various reasons—it could be that we don't want to deal with their tantrums, engage in power struggles when they object, or even because we feel guilty. Wade says, "With Brian, I used to feel like I was simply being unfair by setting and enforcing rules at all times. I felt like his actions were just what could be expected of a child at his age and thought I needed to release the reins a little." We can easily think "kids will be kids" and hold back on setting limits for them because of this but in order to feel secure and safe, children need limits. Regardless of what your child may say or think about the guidelines you have set, they have more to gain now and in the future by adhering to them.

In the real world, that is, the one outside your home, there are rules and there are consequences as well. Explaining how this works to your children starting now will help them to cultivate self-discipline and also learn how to abide by society's stated and unstated rules when the time comes. When you tell your child "no" or set a specific limit for them, you are helping them to understand the concept of boundaries. These boundaries he or she learns at home are their first exposure to the world as they exist out there as well. The fact remains that a time will come when your little one will grow and have to face reality on their own without you being there to guide them. When children do not receive reasonable and adequate exposure to boundaries and rules right from home, it becomes much harder for them to deal with them successfully in social situations. Children will hardly ever admit that they like having rules laid down for them, but they might agree that knowing what is expected of them can be helpful. For us, as parents, the secret to setting boundaries is actually not in how often we say "no" to our children or prevent them from doing certain things but rather in knowing the best way to say "no" to them. While spanking, yelling, and other punitive reactions may work in the meantime, these are majorly based on resentment and fear and will be less effective in the long run.

In setting kind and firm limits for children, love and respect are key ingredients. It can be immensely difficult for us to maintain true respect for our children when we have to set a limit and their emotions are off the hook. That frustrating moment when your child keeps hitting you because you have interrupted his or her playtime to bathe them or when your baby is screeching because you took away their plate after emptying their meal on the ground repeatedly are the times that will put your own capabilities for respect and calmness to the test. However, it is important to remember that just when our kids seem to deserve our respect the least is when they need it the most. Our role as parents is not to find punishments for their mistakes but to show them how to respect limits and handle their emotions productively and healthily. Setting loving limits with respect for them requires as much confidence, neutrality, and firmness as possible. When your child misbehaves, strive to ensure that your responses emanate from a place of connection, empathy, and importantly, love. Children understand limits better when it is communicated to them in direct and simple language rather than long, confusing lectures.

Setting limits for kids helps them to learn appropriate behavior and also allows them to improve some of their skills. If you find yourself holding back from setting a limit for your child, below are five great ways by which doing so can be beneficial for them-

It teaches them self-discipline—Your child's self-discipline skills are enhanced when you set proper limits for them. For example, telling them to pack up their toys to go do their homework is a way of teaching them self-discipline. This helps him or her to realize the importance of being responsible, even though toys may be more fun to play with. One way we can help our children to come up with strategies that impose limits on themselves is by setting a timer as they get dressed in the morning and encouraging them to beat it as they do so.

It keeps them healthy—Children are naturally impulsive and love immediate satisfaction. Setting limits with their eating habits for example will help them to make healthier choices. Without limits, kids are completely fine with eating junk food for the entire day. "When I first started setting limits for Jo, she'd get upset to hear that she couldn't have another cookie or candy and throw tantrums. Later on though, she got better at acting in line with them and would not have more than 2 cookies at once, even without having to be reminded", Sierra says. Setting limits concerning electronics will also promote a healthy lifestyle as many kids are content playing on the computer or watching TV all day.

It shows them that you care—Many times, children will test limits just to see the reactions they can get out of adults around. They want to be reassured that you're in control and can keep their actions in check. When there are negative consequences for broken rules, you prove to them that you won't allow things to get out of control and that you have love for them. For instance, if you tell a teenager that you care about them and that is why they have a curfew, they may be displeased on the surface. At the same time however, this communicates to them that you are ready to invest time and energy into their lives even if you have to bear being seen as a mean parent.

It keeps them safe—With limits, children learn how to keep themselves safe. While he or she may be able to play outside safely, limits about the places they can go when they're playing alone or the things they're allowed to do will be beneficial. They also keep children safe when using the internet and when they start to carry out activities on their own. As children mature, the limits they are given should also expand accordingly. Allow your children to show how responsible they can be with set limits. When they are able to act in line with these limits, it is an indication that they are mature enough to handle even more.

It helps them to cope with uncomfortable emotions—Many parents are guilty of avoiding limits with their kids because they don't want to upset them or make them angry. However, we all would agree that learning how to handle our uncomfortable emotions is a valuable life skill. For this reason, it is best to start helping them to get the hang of it from a tender age. You should not allow your child to spend the entire day in front of the Tv without doing his or her homework simply because denying them of it will make them sad. In fact, healthy limits help you to teach your child healthy ways they can handle their feelings. By showing children how to cope with unpleasant emotions, their abilities to handle the realities of adulthood will be improved.

To set kind and effective limits, here is a general step by step process that you can make use of-

1. **Calm yourself**—After we have tried bringing our children to order with no success, it can be very easy for us to lash out angrily or punish them. However,

the first step to dealing with situations like this is to remind ourselves to stay calm. Before you respond to your child's misbehavior, take some deep breaths to clear your head and decide on the best line of action to follow next.

2. **Acknowledge their feelings or actions**—It is important to set limits for your child's behaviors but not their emotions. Remember that even if children might not always know the best way to communicate and process their needs, all their actions have a reason behind them. Take note of their actions or feelings with statements like "you go so angry that you hit me" or "You seem to be having so much fun jumping on the couch." Doing this helps them to highlight the particular misbehavior that you are trying to set limits on.

3. **Set limits**—After acknowledging the misbehavior, proceed with setting the needed limits. For example, you can tell a child who won't stop jumping on the couch "It's not safe to jump on the couch. I can't allow you to do that. You can sit on it or try jumping on these floor pillows instead." If your child keeps playing with his or her food or spilling it on the floor, tell them "Doing that means you're no longer hungry. Let us take your plate back to the kitchen."

4. **Follow through**—Accept your child's emotional response and empathize with it as you follow through. If appropriate, you can also offer an alternative for them. For the jumping child in the scenario above, move him or her from the couch to the pillows yourself if they still do not budge. Allow

them to cry or throw a tantrum but make sure that you show them empathy. You could say something along the lines of "I know it must be really frustrating, I can tell you were having so much fun on the couch". As for the child who keeps spilling food, remove the plate yourself and move it to the kitchen. Empathize with them by saying something like "I know you want your plate back. It's hard to wait but you'll have your next meal soon." Until it is actually their next mealtime, avoid giving him or her extra snacks to properly enforce the limit you have set for them.

Needless to say, it can be quite challenging to set limits and also maintain them. However, to help you do this effectively with your child, here are 12 valuable tips you can bear in mind-

Be less general—Reduce the chances of ambiguity in your instructions by being direct and specific about what you want your child to do. If your child has a tendency to stall, you could tell him or her to finish a particular task before you enjoy a game or some other fun activity together. Let them know that if the task is not done before a set time, the activity will be skipped for the day.

Pay attention to your nonverbal cues—Your facial expressions and body language when setting limits for children are of great importance as well. When you are serious about enforcing a rule, let your tone communicate that you mean business. Also, try to come down to their level at all times to reduce the chances of them feeling intimidated.

Let them know the consequences of their misbe-

havior—Stating consequences before they even get an opportunity to disobey can be very effective with strong-willed children. Although doing this might require some practice, it works great when you master how to do it. For instance, if your child keeps leaving their bed after their bedtime, you can tell them you will close the door for some minutes if they don't stop. Telling him or her the consequence beforehand helps them to know that they have to remain in bed if they want the door to be open.

Be consistent—Consistency is key when setting boundaries for our children so as to prevent any confusions. Children can easily get confused when we accept and encourage a particular behavior one day and then scold them for it the following day. Your child cannot easily grasp all the workings of social interactions just yet and being consistent is the primary way we can make that easier for them.

Be prepared for their displeasure—Even now when someone tells us "no," it can be quite upsetting for us. The only difference is that we know not to throw tantrums or burst into tears as a result. When you set a limit for your child, don't expect that he or she will act in line with it without getting upset. Allow it to happen but show empathy at the same time. It can be tough for children when they don't get what they want but rest assured that your little one is capable of working through his or her feelings.

Consider posting the rules—Printing out or writing the rules in their bedroom or in the kitchen is one way to help children get used to the idea of rules. When they see them constantly, it helps them to realize that these limits are always there for them to live by.

Think of the bigger picture—Just like us, it is harder for children to cooperate when they are not feeling fine. Before setting a particular limit for your child, ask yourself if they could be ill, hungry, tired, lonely, or anxious. Oftentimes, sorting out these problems first can put an end to their challenging behavior.

Acknowledge their appropriate behavior—Although your child might misbehave from time to time, it is also important to pay attention to the right things they do. Try paying attention to the things that your children are doing well too.

Let your expectations be age-appropriate—As kids develop, their actions and thoughts change too, and your expectations need to be suited to their present stage. For example, a 2-year-old child will likely have difficulty with sharing his or her things while a 5-year-old can be a bit sassy. At each stage of their development, try brushing up on where they currently are and don't expect a 3-year-old to be as willing as a 7-year-old child.

Help out when needed—Sometimes, we think insistence is the best way to get our children to do things, but this is really not the case. We all have been in situations where we find certain tasks so daunting that we give up on it almost as soon as we start doing it. Similarly too, it is possible for kids to get overwhelmed with a particular task and what they need is our support in times like this. For instance, telling your child "let's clean up your room together" when it seems too overwhelming for them will help them learn to handle the task better.

Remember that there are no good or bad children

—Children and adults alike behave in both acceptable and unacceptable ways. This is the natural order of things and so we should avoid tagging our children as "bad" because of their misbehavior. This does more in creating a negative self-image than it does in improving said behavior.

Don't use bribes—Encouraging cooperative behavior and bribing children to get a desired effect are really not the same thing. A bribe is simply a child's reward for doing what we want them to and if we do this, children can learn manipulation quickly and even end up outsmarting us.

It is crucial to set limits for our children because it helps them to learn the way life works in general and that not all their actions are acceptable. We need to be careful to make sure that the limits we set for them are not against them but for their own benefit. Setting kind and firm limits help to ensure the wellbeing of every family member and also promote cooperation. With limits, your family life will be much easier, and you can rest assured that you are providing your child with the guidelines they need to develop properly.

The major goal of setting limits is to curb undesired behavior in our children. However, the fact remains that children will misbehave at one point in time or the other whether through lies, tantrums, disobedience, or some other action. In situations like this, what is the next line of action? The next chapter will highlight common child behavior problems as well as the best way to respond to them.

Chapter Summary

- Rules help children to learn how to act in different situations.
- Remember that children need our respect most in situations where they seem to be most undeserving of it.
- When setting limits for your child, make sure that they are for their own benefit and not against them.
- Rules keep children safe; help them to know that you care; teach them positive coping mechanisms; help them to be disciplined and keep them healthy.

In the next chapter you will learn about some common child behavior problems and how to respond to children's misbehavior the right way.

7

RESPOND TO MISBEHAVIOR

Before we can learn the best ways to respond to our children's misbehavior, we first need to understand the reason behind it. Learning why they misbehave in the first place will give us needed insight on how we can try preventing such problems. Did you know that a child who misbehaves is one who feels discouraged? When children feel like out of place or like they are not significant, there is a higher chance of them displaying undesired behavior. They then misbehave with the wrong notion that this is the only way they can achieve that sense of belonging and significance that they crave.

Most times, young children do not yet have properly developed communication skills and therefore cannot directly say what they need. If they are bored, tired, or hungry, it is common for them to misbehave. Little tricks such as keeping a few toys with you to prevent boredom or having some snacks handy can help them to show their best behavior. Children who have strong emotions or are under some sort of stress can also misbehave as it can be difficult for them to remember the rules during times like this. Even positive changes can be hard for children to deal with and so we need to space out the changes we make around a certain time. With our daily commitments, it can be easy for us to get caught up and starve our kids of needed attention. Even though they might not know the best way to ask for our attention, the fact remains that they need it. When you get home from work each day, do you rush to check your mail and get dinner ready? How about sparing some minutes to sit with your little one and talk about what happened during their day instead? Seemingly insignificant things like this are beneficial in helping to keep misbehavior at bay.

Sometimes, children will exhibit behavioral problems when they do not have the necessary social or problem-solving skills to deal with certain situations. For example, a child may hit another child because they're interested in the same toy or refuse to clean up his or her room because they're confused about some toys not fitting into the toy box. Times like this, it is best to show the child in question the right way to behave instead of just giving them a consequence. To encourage proper development, children need to be taught alternatives to their misbehavior to enable them to learn from their mistakes. Asides from this, watching others and imitating them in the major way children learn how to behave. Even if we do all we can to set good behavioral examples for them, they can still pick up the wrong kind of behavior from their peers in school or from what they see on TV. Apart from role modelling positive behavior for our kids, we also need to try to limit the amount of exposure they have to unhealthy behavior in real life, video games, and on TV. Reduce the amount of screen time your young child gets and even when they do watch TV, let it be shows that encourage good morals.

Generally, children will misbehave with any of these four goals in mind-

1. Attention—In the mind of a misbehaving child, he or she can only feel a sense of belonging when they are the center of attention.
2. Misguided power—This is when children think that their sense of belonging comes only when they are in charge of their own decisions or do not let adults boss them around.
3. Revenge—A misbehaving child who is out to get revenge will believe that even though they don't feel like they belong, at least they can get even.
4. Assumed inadequacy—In this case, they lack a true sense of belonging and resort to giving up and being left to do whatever they please.

In order for you to identify the particular mistaken goal your child has in mind, you need to pay attention to the way you, as an adult, react and the way the child reacts.

The Child Who Needs Attention

In this situation, the parent is likely to feel guilty, irritated, worried, or annoyed while the child will react by trying some other means of getting your attention or stopping their misbehavior temporarily and then resuming it later on. This child is actually trying to tell you to notice or involve them and it is best to pay attention to what he or she needs and not their behavior.

How to Deal With It

Give your child quality attention during the day—We need to make time during the day to give our children one-on-one attention. Include social time with your child into your daily routine.

Discuss with them beforehand—To prevent the chances of misbehavior due to lack of attention, it is best to speak to your child in advance while you are both calm. Let them know the expectations you have for them and what will happen if they do misbehave. For instance, if your child keeps interrupting you while you're engaged in conversations, let them know that it is not okay for them to interrupt unless there's a real emergency. Train them on what a true emergency is and when it is acceptable for them to interrupt you.

Show them the right way to get your attention—You can create a sort of signal with your child that he or she can use if they need you when there's no emergency. For example, they could touch your hand gently to show that they need to interrupt you when you have a moment. Older children could even slide you a written note or draw a picture of what they need. Doing this shows children that sometimes interruptions are allowed during non-emergencies but should be done respectfully. You can also role play this at home to help your child get the hang of it before they actually need to do so.

Let them know the consequences—Tell your child the consequences of misbehaving in advance. If he or she tries seeking your attention in a disrespectful way, let them know that you will ignore them and walk away.

The Child with Misguided Power

In this situation, parents might feel angry, challenged, defeated, or threatened. The child's reaction to this is to continue with the same behavior, agree to stop but continue with it, or become defiant. What the child is actually trying to communicate is that they need to be given choices or allowed to help out too.

How to Deal With It

Get rid of the idea of winning—In any situation where there's a winner, someone has to be the loser. When children have the notion that they lose when they give in to your instructions, it all becomes a competition to them. Remember that the goal is not for our children to lose but to learn proper behavior. With compromise, teamwork, and collaboration, we can use such opportunities to teach our children valuable life skills and promote a healthy relationship with them.

Allow them to make choices too—Children need to be

able to make their own choices and have control over certain decisions. With a bit of control, children feel powerful and useful and are less likely to engage in power struggles. Allowing them to have a say in what meal to make for dinner, whether they want to do their homework or clean their room first is a way to share power with them on our own terms.

Avoid getting into power struggles—Bowing out in situations like this is effective in managing your child's misbehavior. To have a tug of war, you need to have two participants and when you do not partake, your child will have nobody to fight against. Allowing ourselves to react or get into arguments with them will only give them that sense of power that they want.

The Child Who Wants Revenge

Here, a parent might feel disgusted, disappointed, hurt, or be disbelieving. A child who is seeking revenge will react by resorting to destructive behavior, intensify his or her misbehavior, or say hurtful things. Such a child is actually trying to let adults around know that he or she is hurting and needs their feelings to be validated.

How to Deal With It

Be empathetic—In situations like this, it is important to let children know that hurt feelings are normal and that expressing them is completely okay. Work with them to come up with positive words and ways to identify and express these negative emotions. Responding with empathy will not only help your young one feel heard but valued as well.

Encourage them to own up to their actions—Although hurt feelings are normal, children need to be taught to take responsibility for the things they do asides from learning to express them. Help your child to understand the effects their words and actions have on other people by apologizing when needed, cleaning up their mess, or replacing items. Doing this is a good way of teaching our children respect and citizenship.

Set boundaries—The boundaries of your parent-child relationship need to be clearly defined. Talk to your child about respectful ways to communicate with people and how important it is to respect people and owned items.

Work on keeping the peace—Although we might be tempted to lash out at our kids or strike back when they hurt us in some way, it is best to remain calm. By handling our own feelings properly, we teach our children to be considerate of another person's feelings and also deal with tough situations in a dignified manner.

The Child Who Feels Inadequate

Parents may despair, feel inadequate or feel hapless in such situations while the child's reaction would be to act out, become passive, retreat even further into his or her shell, be non-responsive, or show no signs of improvement. This child is actually trying to tell his or her parents to not give up on them and give them just a little push.

How to Deal With It

Accept them for who they are—We all aren't perfect—how much more young children? Setting unreasonably high standards for them will definitely result in their failure to measure up. The best thing to do is to create an environment where imperfection, mistakes and failures are okay. Help your child to realize that failure is okay as it is a good way for us to learn and grow.

Be attentive and present—When children know that you are present and responsive to their needs, it helps them to feel safe and loved. This in turn makes it easier for them to seek comfort or help from you when they need to. Teach your child that it's okay for them to need some alone time to tackle their uncomfortable feelings. However, this alone time should be treated as more of a retreat with a soothing activity than a punishment.

Breaking rules and going against the norm to test limits are common traits in children as this is the major way they distinguish between appropriate and inappropriate behavior. Below are 5 common misbehaviors that children tend to display from time to time and how to respond to such behaviors.

Tantrums

Your child's temper tantrums may come up suddenly and fiercely at times. You and your child may be having a good time grocery shopping together one minute and the next, he or she may be whining and screaming at the top of their lungs because you won't let them add a set of battery cases to the cart. This is especially common in kids aged between 1 and 3 and while you may worry that your child is trying to manipulate you, it likely means that their frustration is causing a meltdown. With limited communication skills, children cannot express their true wants or feelings and get frustrated as a result.

Solutions

Keep your cool—A tantrum can be a very difficult situation to handle. Apart from screaming or kicking, some children may even throw things or hold their breath for several minutes. At this time, children cannot listen to reason and will negatively respond to your threats or yells. In fact, the more you shout at them to stop throwing a tantrum, the higher their chances of getting even wilder. You have a better chance of calming your child by staying with him or her while they undergo this period of frustration. This wave of emotion they're feeling can frighten them and knowing you're close by will help them to avoid feeling abandoned.

Make use of time-ins occasionally—Time-ins can help during especially intense tantrums when other methods seem not to work. Using time-ins from time to time can help children to work through their feelings better. Children can learn self-soothing when they are placed in a different spot for a short period of time. Many of us are familiar with timeouts during which a child is restricted to a particular area alone. However, these can be harmful as imposing our will on children is detrimental and does not provide them with an opportunity to learn. Sometimes, all children need is a break from a particular situation and it is best to take them somewhere else where they can calm down. Instead of time-outs, make use of the "Remove and Redirect" strategy where you remove the object, remove the child, redirect the child's attention, and redirect their activity. Let them know what you're doing and why and be sure to remind them that you'll be nearby during their time-in. Stay with them as they work through those difficult feelings and emotions.

Talk to them after the tantrum—When your child is calmer, hold them close and discuss what happened with them in very basic terms. Acknowledge their frustration by helping them to put their feelings into words when they can't. Help them to know that expressing themselves in words and not through tantrums will help them to get better results.

Lying

Young children have a hard time distinguishing fantasy from reality and might not be able to understand the concepts of being truthful and lying just yet. Sometimes, kids simply forget the things they do or wish so much that they didn't do it that they somehow convince themselves that they didn't. Other times, their creativity undergoes rapid development, and their active imaginations leads them to thinking that what they believe is the truth. Lying in children could also stem from what can be referred to as the "angel syndrome" during which they realize that their parents think they are infallible and start to believe so too. Such a child would believe that he or she is loved cause they're so good and since good children do not leave crayon marks on the wall, they deny having anything to do with it.

Solutions

Build their trust—Children need to know that you trust them and that they can trust in you as well. They should be taught that honesty is the best policy, and we can role model this too by avoiding telling half-truths. For example, telling a child their shot during a checkup won't hurt will definitely backfire because they'll find out sooner or later that it does. Try keeping your word at all times and apologizing for broken promises when you can't fulfill them. It is also important to avoid scolding them when they do tell the truth as positive reinforcement helps them to see the value in truth-telling.

Avoid accusations—Rather than "Why did you leave all these crayon marks on the wall?" say something like "I wonder who left these crayon marks on the wall. I wish someone would help me to clean them up." With children, we need to structure our comments in ways that make it easier for them to own up than to deny their actions.

Go easy on the rules and expectations—Children may not be able to follow or understand your rules or expectations when they're too many. When your child feels overburdened or weighed down, they may feel like lying is the best way to avoid your disappointment.

Aggressive Behavior

While it is normal for children to get angry, the problem results when they become violent or resort to aggressive behavior. Developing impulse control, frustration, budding communication skills and a strong desire for independence are some of the primary causes of this behavior in children. Aggression is also a behavior that children can pick up from the environments they are exposed to—be it at home or in school.

Solutions

Give consistent discipline—Try to respond to each episode of your child's aggressive behavior the same way as much as possible. By having a predictable response each time he or she displays aggression, you create a pattern for them that they will eventually recognize. As time goes on, they will realize that consequences await them if they misbehave.

Take note of what they watch—Media such as digital games and cartoons for young children can contain hitting, shouts, threats and shoving. The more we expose our children to this, the more they cultivate the habit of being aggressive. If your child has a tendency to be aggressive, choose only media that promotes the right values and is age appropriate.

Reinforce good behavior—Children need to be given attention when they behave positively too and not only when they misbehave. For example, if he or she asks for a turn with a toy instead of simply grabbing it from another child's hands, encourage the behavior. You could even offer to play with them so that they realize the power in verbalizing what they want instead of biting, kicking, or hitting.

Disobedience or Backtalk

With younger children, it could seem adorable when they talk back or give a funny response to your instructions. However, it can be unnerving when a 7- or 8-year-old child shouts "no" whenever you ask him or her to do something. Children will sometimes hear selectively and will only pay attention to the instructions that favor them—your child may hear when you call them for dinner, but their ears will fail them when it's bath time. Times like this, it can be a struggle to remain calm and not dish out some punitive actions. The truth remains however, that at one point in time or the other, children will test limits.

Solutions

Set limits for them—Rather than making threats, introduce limits to your child and let him or her know the consequences for their improper behavior. You could say something like "If you do not do your homework before dinner, game night will be cancelled for today." You could also use the "when... then" method of warning by telling them what they need to do and what will happen after it is done. You could say something along the lines of "When you clean up your room, then you can watch TV." If they still do not comply, follow up with a consequence. If this is done consistently, children will learn to obey your instructions as soon as you give them.

Pay attention to their reactions—You can choose to ignore backtalk if your child still follows your instructions all the same. Even if they talk back, you can appreciate that they followed your instructions even though they didn't want to. Later on, you can make time to explain to them that while it is normal to be angry, speaking to you disrespectfully is not acceptable.

Avoid impulsive responses—Try not to respond impulsively when your child disobeys you or talks back. It is best to allow him or her to calm down and then address their words or inactions. Calmly let them know the kinds of behaviors that are acceptable and those that are not.

Laziness

Sometimes your child may not be interested in participating in anything at all be it cleaning, playing, schoolwork or any other activity. In cases like this, it can be tricky to get them motivated enough to want to do anything. The best way to do this is by finding ways for them to get motivated on their own as this is more effective than driving them to do things.

Solutions

Don't be forceful—As mentioned earlier in this book, choices help children to feel more in control and like they have a say over matters that concern them. Instead of forcing children to take up a particular activity, we need to provide them with options they can choose from. If your child gets to choose something on their own, there is a higher chance that he or she will be more interested in it.

Try to find the underlying reason—It is good to take a step back and try to see the cause of your child's laziness or lack of motivation. Could it be that you're forcing them to do something they really do not want to do? Bear in mind that your child is a separate individual and the only way you can truly know what they want or motivates them is by asking.

Make daily chores more fun—Younger children can be encouraged to partake in chores by adding a bit of fun to it. Come up with fun creative ways of doing things that will keep your child motivated. For example, you can create a competition to see who makes their bed first, who folds the highest number of clothes, and so on.

Children will randomly misbehave once in a while and we would do well to address it from a place of love and empathy. These misbehaviors serve as a learning opportunity for us, as parents and for our children as well. With consistent discipline, we help kids to learn about rules and also show them appropriate lines of actions. At the same time, we need to realize that periodic regression is normal for kids and your child may exhibit unacceptable behavior even after complying for months. These phases are normal and may be a developmental process he or she needs to experience. Try to understand your child's motive for an unhealthy behavior and provide guidance as needed. There's no need to get anxious about this—by using calm and consistent responses, most issues will be resolved in a short while.

Times when children refuse to adhere to the rules and instructions we lay down, it may become necessary to give them consequences for their actions. However, what kinds of consequences do we give them and how can we enforce them properly? In the following chapter, we'll take a look at natural and logical consequences as well as how to follow through with them.

Chapter Summary

- Taking time to find out why our children misbehave will help us know how to prevent such occurrences later.
- A child who seeks attention is actually asking you to involve or take notice of them.
- A child who tries to gain power really wants you to allow them help out or give them choices.
- A vengeful child is one that is hurting and wants you to validate their feelings.
- A child who feels inadequate wants his or her parents to give them just a little nudge and not give up on them.

In the next chapter you will learn the difference between natural and logical consequences and how to enforce them with your children.

8

LOVE AND LOGIC CONSEQUENCES

Earlier in this book, we established the fact that discipline means teaching our children and not punishing them. The traditional method of discipline that many of us were brought up with involves our own parents giving us rewards for our obedience and punishments when we disobey them. As studies and research have progressed however, we have seen that this traditional method of discipline can lead to potential problems in our children. Apart from hindering children from learning how to make their own decisions, rewards and punishments also suggest to children that they are only expected to behave appropriately when authority figures are present. A better way of child discipline is to implement natural and logical consequences as this helps in raising resilient children rather than compliant ones. Consequences can be helpful in adjusting a child's behaviors as and when needed because they separate the child from the bad choice they made and focus more on the misbehavior than the child. They also eliminate the possibility of punishment or anger as they will teach your child healthy lines of actions to take instead of you having to yell or react emotionally. Consequences help children to be responsible for their actions and also allow them to make choices. Aside from these, they also help to prevent punishing, judging, or shaming the erring child.

As the name implies, natural consequences occur as a result of your child's decisions or actions without any interference or input. An example of this kind of consequence would be a child refusing to wear a jacket when it's cold and then feeling cold as a result. Another example would be a child's refusal to put laundry in the basket as they are told and then having only their clothes in the basket washed. They may not work well with younger children as they may not be able to understand that their behavior directly leads to the consequence. On the other hand, a logical consequence is one that a parent or caregiver gives to a child who breaks a rule or misbehaves. This consequence should ideally be linked to the unhealthy behavior that you are trying to curb. Examples include taking a toy away for a period of time from a child who's been told not to play with it or removing his or her bike riding privileges if he or she refuses to wear a helmet. Generally, logical consequences are better in ensuring the safety and health of children than natural ones. For example, allowing a child to ride his or her bicycle without a helmet for them to experience the natural consequence would be inappropriate. It would also be downright neglectful to allow the natural consequence of cavities forming in the mouth of a child who refuses to brush their teeth. However, with both natural and logical consequences, the goal remains helping children to learn from their mistakes and make better decisions next time. These consequences can be implemented when children engage in food-related power struggles, have problems with personal responsibility, repeat certain actions even after you have intervened in the past, or display selfish behavior.

It can be tricky to decide the right kind of consequence for certain situations, but it really depends on the circumstances at a given time. When using logical consequences, it is important to make use of the 3 R's—they need to be relatable, respectful, and reasonable. A consequence being relatable means that it is related to the behavior your child has displayed while also respecting the child as a person and not involving blaming or shaming. Lastly, a consequence that is reasonable should make sense from your perspective as a parent and your child's own as well. If a child does not complete their homework and has issues at school as a result, it would be more reasonable to discuss with them about reducing their playtime than grounding them for a month. There is also a need to consider your child's safety and the consequences that will be in their best interests. Natural consequences are usually more helpful when they take place immediately. If your child refuses to wear a seatbelt while they drive, for instance, a logical consequence of taking their keys away would be more appropriate than a natural one.

How Can I Use Natural and Logical Consequences?

Parents need to ensure that the consequence they give their kids for misbehaving relates to the improper behavior. In order for children to get the message clearly and properly, the consequence needs to fit the mistake. For example, denying a child of dessert because they don't pick up their toys after playtime will not do much. In a case like this, holding on to their toys for a set period of time will be more sensible and effective. The consequence you enforce should relate to the particular behavior you want to discourage. With natural consequences, you simply allow the consequences to play out on their own after you have warned your child in advance of an outcome that is less than desirable. The best thing about natural consequences is that they are life's best teachers and instead of parents having to do any lecturing, the experience teaches lessons by itself. For instance, a natural consequence for a child who has been warned in advance against forgetting their lunch repeatedly would be him or her having to figure out an alternative on their own. In this case, they would either have to be hungry for some hours or share their friend's lunch.

It can be hard for parents to sit back and let natural consequences follow because we don't want to see our children go hungry or feel uncomfortable in any way. However, you need to realize that you won't always be able to bail them out in real-life situations where there are consequences. Children are more likely to make better decisions when they grow when they learn to face consequences right from childhood. Before you allow a natural or logical consequence to play out, it is important to let your child know in advance that you'll no longer be involved as allowing it to happen without prior information would be simply unfair. If your child frequently forgets his or her lunch or homework at home, for example, here is one way to go about it-

Start a conversation about said behavior with them when you're both in a good mood. Emphasize that they're old enough to remember their homework or lunchbox on their own. You could say something like "Therefore, I will no longer bring your lunchbox or homework to school if you forget it. You'll either have to be hungry or look for a way out on your own. However, I believe in you and I am confident that you can remember it." As their success is of utmost importance, we could even take extra steps to help them do this. You could say "Since I will no longer be reminding you about this, what do you think you can do to help you remember?" This way, we show our children that their welfare still matters to us. We could assist by putting a reminder on his or her phone or putting a sign on the door for them to see as they leave home. Together, brainstorm on some solutions and see what your child comes up with.

Emphasizing that having a certain privilege implies that they have to be responsible about it is another way to make use of consequences. When your child knows that he or she can lose the privilege of having certain items if they don't take responsibility for it, there's a lesser chance that they will misbehave. Monica, mother to 6-year-old Shannon says, "My daughter had the habit of leaving her crayons laying around and losing them as a result. My first reaction was to pick up another set of crayons from the store but now, she knows that they will be taken away for some time or placed out of her reach if she does not care for them properly." Doing this can be beneficial even with non-tangible things—for instance, if a child refuses to speak to you with respect, they lose the privilege of you listening to them. You could say something like "I would love to talk to you about this, but you have to speak with respect. When you're ready to do that, I'll be in my room."

One way to make use of consequences with children is to remind them that they have choices. Offer them choices that won't harm their emotional health and are okay for you as well. Instead of using threats to drive home your point, tell them that they need to take a break to calmly think about the misbehavior they have displayed. For example, instead of yelling at your younger child because he or she keeps kicking their sibling, follow through with the consequence of putting themselves in their place to understand how it feels to be kicked. When they are ready to play nicely, they can then join the family and resume playtime.

Allowing children to choose the consequence of their actions can also be effective as they are more likely to participate this way. As much as is possible, let your child get involved in choosing the consequence—you might be shocked to find out that he or she may even come up with a better one than you would if they are given the opportunity. This way, you can be sure that your child will actually face the consequences on their own when they don't act in accordance with expected behavior. It is also important to follow through with consequences immediately after the misbehavior and not later. This helps children to create a link between their misbehavior and the consequence.

Logical consequences are created by adults and we either delay a privilege, deny it, or ask them to make amends for misbehavior. For example, a child who doesn't wear his or her helmet repeatedly can lose the privilege of riding their bike for the day. Before we apply logical consequences too, prior information is important. If your child forgets to clean up his or her blocks each time after playing with them, you could say something along these lines— "I noticed that you forget to clean up your blocks every time you play with them and leave them on the floor for days. Playing with your blocks is a privilege and it comes with certain responsibilities so our rule for playing with them is that you have to pick them up when you're done. I expect that you will put them away and clean them up after you play with them. I'm pretty sure you can do this, but the choice is yours. I'll have to take them away if you decide not to." If there's a need to follow through, you can empathize with them by saying "I know it must be very hard for you to not have your blocks with you, but this is an opportunity for you to learn. I'm sure that you'll make a better choice tomorrow."

Consequences should be enforced privately when possible— remember that children likely feel bad on their own already after misbehaving. Following through with consequences when other people are around will only add to their humiliation and shame.

When you set a consequence for a certain behavior, consistency is important so as to leave no room for confusion on your child's part. If you tell your child their crayons will be withheld if they do not pack them up after use today and then permit it tomorrow, it will only throw your child into confusion about what you truly expect from them.

How often do you nag your child about their past misbehavior? Statements like "You always jump on the couch," "You never listen to instructions," and so on will only deal a blow to their developing self-esteem. Appreciation and positive reinforcement are better appreciated by children than nagging. Pay attention to what is going on in the present and let what they have done in the past remain in the past. Avoid criticizing them and encourage them when they display proper behavior.

Just like in all other aspects of child upbringing, patience plays a vital role. Using consequences for your child may not be effective right away but if you stick to doing so, your child will get the hang of it eventually. Resorting to the use of traditional methods because it seems to be taking 'too long' will only be disadvantageous to your child. Take things slow with them and allow them to learn the benefits of having consequences for their actions.

Using natural and logical consequences for children as disciplinary strategies are more effective than the use of threats of punishments. Apart from separating the child from their misbehavior, they provide valuable lessons for them which they can use to make better choices in the future. However, it is vital to give your child a heads-up regardless of the kind of consequence you want to apply to ensure fairness. There has been a lot of debate on the best methods for disciplining children right from time. Is spanking or slapping the best way to go? What do you think? The fact remains that the best discipline methods are those that focus more on the child's learning and development than on the improper action they have taken. In the next chapter, let us take a look at some positive and respectful discipline methods that you can use for your child as well as how you can implement them.

Chapter Summary

- Natural and logical consequences help raise resilient children instead of compliant ones.
- A natural consequence is a direct result of a child's choices and requires no input or interference from an adult.
- A logical consequence is one that is administered to a misbehaving child by a parent or caregiver.
- Consequences need to be Relatable, Respectful and Reasonable.

In the next chapter you will learn recommended positive discipline methods for children and how you can implement them.

9

APPLY RESPECTFUL DISCIPLINE METHODS

When tackling children's improper behavior, the most important thing is teaching them the right way to behave and not punishing them for their misbehavior. We would all agree that we want our children to be better people and that is what should be given paramount attention. There's no doubt that raising children takes a lot and steering them in the right direction can be much trickier than it sounds. Sadly, nobody is born with a guide on being a good parent and there are times when we'll have to make the best choices that will help raise productive and decent kids. It can be helpful to know healthy techniques for disciplining our children to help keep them guided. The first time your child behaves in a way that needs correction, you may wonder what the best and most effective way of disciplining them is. A lot of parents try reasoning with their kids but later resort to spanking or hitting them when they refuse to act in line. The use of force suddenly becomes an alternative and later, a dangerous habit. Over the years, spanking children becomes a method that almost always produces the desired results, but the truth remains that doing so is not healthy for them, physically and emotionally. In fact, this method does more harm to children in the long run than good.

In 2014, as many as 38 different countries in the world had banned spanking as a means of disciplining or punishing children—and for good reason too. Hitting children or yelling at them when they misbehave gives them the false notion that hitting other people who do wrong things is acceptable too. With their impressionable minds, they will see this as an acceptable option and pick it up right from a tender age. Spanking your child will set off a feeling of fear in them and they will believe that they can rightfully hit people younger than them. Asides from the physical hurt you inflict on your child when you hit him or her, there is also the emotional pain which is even much more detrimental. Hitting children and regularly telling them they're bad can have damaging effects that last even up till adulthood. He or she will assume that they're bad children and will have no respect for themselves as they grow older. Corporal punishment is a method that can leave emotional scars in the minds of our young ones and should therefore be avoided at all costs.

For children to grow up to be disciplined adults, we, as parents, need to lay down the right example. Model positivity and discipline and your kids will likely do the same too. By creating a healthy and positive environment for them, we lay down the foundation for their success. We need to always exercise some patience to understand the reason behind our children's misbehavior. It could simply be that your young one just wants to feel significant and like he or she belongs in your family. At all times, try to correct with love and patience instead of simply ordering them around.

Below are 7 of the most positive and effective methods for disciplining your child to keep him or her in line as opposed to corporal punishment-

Always let them know why—If you give your child an instruction or set a certain expectation for them, "because I said so" is not the best reason to give. Bear in mind that children are only starting to learn how the world works and giving them explanations is a great way to help them do this. When they ask questions and you only tell them off, you cause them to get frustrated. If you tell your child to set the table and they ask you why, let them know it's because it's a nice gesture and you want the whole family together for dinner. Giving children reasons for certain things is also beneficial when they misbehave as simply saying "I don't want you to play in the yard now" gives them zero information. How about "I don't want you to play in the yard now because it's raining, and you'll likely catch a cold?" By providing kids with the information they need, they learn why they probably shouldn't engage in said behavior in the first place.

Connect with them—If you and a random stranger give the same instruction to your child, there is a much higher chance that he or she will listen to you than a stranger. This is because for children to listen to adults, they need to feel a sense of connection to them. This can be a good thing as we don't want children listening to random strangers anyway. However, it is important to use this knowledge to our advantage as well. In order to truly gain their cooperation, we need to build a strong connection with them. This is where punishment can be found lacking as it negatively affects your connection with your child and puts you at odds with him or her. In turn, the probability of them listening to you is significantly lowered. If you find that your child is misbehaving in some way, create the chance for a little one-on-one time to connect with them. As little as 20 minutes of dedicated and distraction-free time with children on a daily basis can help to make that bond even stronger.

Teach them to express their emotions the right way—Many times when children misbehave, they actually have valid underlying emotions even if they don't handle them the right way. By showing children proper ways of expressing their emotions right from a tender age, it becomes easier for us to know the real reason behind their behaviors and how to address it. For instance, instead of your child stomping into the house after school looking upset, he or she would rather say something like "I got back from school and there was nobody waiting for me as I left the bus. Seeing nobody there got me scared." In a situation like this, parents are better equipped to deal with the child's worries. Helping your child to learn how to express himself or herself will reduce their chances of misbehaving as a means of communication.

More "Yes", less "No"—Naturally, children are curious little beings and exploring their surroundings is how they make discoveries about the world. Constantly turning them down or reprimanding them for doing things will only inhibit their natural curiosity. As they grow older, they need some level of freedom to express their individuality even though this has to be on well-defined terms. Creating an environment that allows them to safely explore will be of great benefit to them. If you have a younger child, you can try placing breakable or dangerous items out of their reach so you don't have to tell them "no" all the time. Asides from encouraging their curiosity, you also get more peace of mind with the knowledge that they're nowhere near an area they shouldn't be. For older kids, you need to be clear about the things that are acceptable and those that aren't. For instance, telling your child "Yes, you can watch TV but if you stay up past your bedtime, there will be no screen time for 3 days" will likely motivate them to practice healthy sleep habits rather than denying them of watching TV altogether. When parents sparingly make use of the word "no", children have a higher chance of paying attention when you do use it.

Lead, don't control—With our kids, being the leader and not the controller is a more effective discipline method. Rather than controlling others, good leaders set people up for success. Regardless of age or size, we all want to be respected and when children feel respected, they want to cooperate. When your child is acting out, it is important to take a step back to make sure that you are leading them and not just controlling. This way, we make it possible for them to grow into happy and healthy adults. When we present ourselves as allies, children will behave well on their own. Making use of punishments or getting mad at them will only produce results out of fear and children who behave properly out of intimidation haven't really learned good behavior. They are only doing so as a means of self-preservation in the face of a threat. Asking your child "What do we have to do to be squeaky clean and smell good?" will definitely yield better results than commanding them to go have a bath.

Don't use harsh words—Aside from physical punishments like spanking, we also need to avoid harsh verbal punishments when correcting our children. Shaming children or yelling at them can greatly increase stress hormones to the point of altering their brain structure. Even if you're generally warm and nurturing towards your child, the use of toxic and harsh words can negatively affect their mental health and behavior. True, we can get so frustrated sometimes that we say things we don't really mean in the heat of the moment, but positive language should always be our go-to. Instead of chiding them, use the right word to steer them in the right direction. Statements like "let's give this a try," "How about if we do this instead?' and so on are more beneficial than those like "Don't do that!"

No Shaming—Let's say your child has just done something they shouldn't have, and you want them to see the faults in their actions, what do you do? Do you shame them for it to pass your point across? Certain phrases and statements have shaming effects and make children feel bad about themselves. Apart from reinforcing their identity as people who behave in a particular way, it is also disadvantageous to their self-esteem. If you tell your child he or she is acting like a baby, this is what they will absorb and will act even more like one. Whatever you say to your child is what they will start to think about themselves and also act accordingly. In his or her young mind, why should they not pick on other children if you call them a bully? Or act like a slob if you refer to them as one? Parents need to strive to let their kids know what behavior is inappropriate without shaming them in the process. Statements like "You're 7 years old, stop acting like a baby!" or "Why don't you ever listen? It's really not so hard!" should be avoided as much as possible when disciplining our children.

In the end, none of us are perfect but we can always strive to be better parents. There will be mistakes along the way but there will also be more opportunities for you to make use of positive discipline choices. Even if we don't know how to perfectly respond to every situation, bearing these methods in mind will increase our chances of doing so. If you've been making use of traditional methods up until this point, it can be overwhelming to start introducing positive discipline methods to your child. However, the key lies in listening to them more than you talk at them—when your child is able to comfortably express themselves with you taking it all in, there is a higher chance of them cooperating. The next time your child misbehaves, take a step back to calm down and discipline them positively and respectfully.

The family home can be likened to a boat with its rowers in it —everyone has a role to play in making sure that it keeps moving and that it moves smoothly as well. Including our children, we all have to contribute and play our roles. In the following chapter, let us take a look at how we can get our children to play their part in the home and help them remain motivated.

Chapter Summary

- The most important thing is showing children how to behave and not punishing them for their misbehavior.
- Spanking is detrimental to a child's emotional and physical wellbeing.
- The use of corporal punishment reduces your value as a parent and disconnects your child from you.
- To get the hang of respectful discipline methods, start by listening to your children and giving needed attention.

In the next chapter you will learn how you can get your children to contribute and play their part in the home.

10

FROM COMPLAINING TO CONTRIBUTING

It is only right that since children add to the mess in the house, they should also contribute to helping clean it up. Apart from making the load of cleaning much lighter for you, this will also help them to grow into adults that are emotionally healthy. Kids need to feel that their contributions are important too and one great way by which parents can help with this is by allowing them to do certain house chores too. Apart from being a part of family life and helping to keep the home in shape, chores also teach children to be responsible. With teamwork, children learn to cooperate and also value another person's viewpoint. In the case of chores, your young one's contribution will help the family have a more organized and cleaner living space which in turn gives the whole family a sense of satisfaction and pride. Taking part in chores also encourages children to compromise and take turns, which are vital skills that will come in handy as they grow older. A lot of parents get frustrated when they assign chores to their children, yet the children do not stay on track with them. However, there are ways we can make chores more fun for children and increase their chances of being willing to partake.

For one, the chore you give to your child has to be age-appropriate and match the abilities of the child in question. Although even very young children can help out and feel useful, it is not all chores that they will be able to handle. For example, your little 4-year-old will likely not be able to handle doing laundry just yet. Activities that require few skills such as helping to rinse vegetables and so on would be much more appropriate. Take time and energy to show them how things are done and where they should go instead of assuming that they will know. If you want your child to put away his or her toys, show them how to if they've never done it before. This way, they learn to do things the right way on their own and also learn the advantages of organizing in other areas of their lives as well.

In order to make it easier for children to help with chores, we need to break it down into very basic steps for them. Asking a 5-year-old child to help you clean up after dinner is a pretty vague concept in their little minds and involves too many steps. On the other hand, breaking it down by telling them to bring the plates after which you'll scrape them and then place them in the washer will help them learn the process while helping out. Teamwork is also a key aspect of assigning chores to children as it presents you with the opportunity of connecting with them. By involving them in decisions and allowing them to choose between folding the clothes and getting out the detergent for instance, we invite them to enjoy the benefits and fun of working together.

A visual chore chart could also come in handy in motivating your child to do their chores. You can create one or make use of an online template and keep it somewhere visible—this could be a central location like the kitchen or dining area. Highlight the chores to be done and you could even add the name of the person assigned to each chore as well. It is important to rotate each chore if possible so that nobody feels stuck with a particular task.

It is best to avoid tying your child's chores to a certain privilege as this can easily lead to a boycott. For example, if you give your 11-year-old child the choice of skipping their turn on doing the dishes if they pass up on their allowance, they might resort to doing this frequently. Asides from a chore boycott, tying chores to privileges can also remove the positive feeling of helping out in the home. We also need to accept any imperfections in the chores our children help out with as the main goal is to help them grow. Your child may not fold clothes or clean up the living room as perfectly as you would, but their efforts count for something too. Appreciate their attempts and encourage them, instead of criticizing.

It can be even harder to get older kids and teenagers to help out regularly but with the right training, this can be achieved. Don't give up on your child and create time to explain why they need to help with chores. Let them know that juggling deadlines, schoolwork, housework, and other aspects of their lives will help them learn how to prioritize and manage their time which will be useful to them in the working world. Avoid nagging them and complaining about having to do things by yourself as there is a lesser chance of getting your child on board that way.

Genuinely appreciating your children when they help out without you having to remind them can also motivate them to be more dedicated towards their chores. Bella, mother to 6-

and 4-year-old Dylan and Arya says, "When my children willingly help out without having to be reminded, I sometimes give out little treats like ice cream. Although they are expected to regularly follow their chores, I like them to know that their efforts are noticed and appreciated." For children who enjoy an element of surprise, you can make doing chores more fun by writing chores on little pieces of paper or ice cream sticks and letting them pick one. These can be categorized by the type of task or room they get assigned to for children to feel like they're actually making a choice. If they agree, siblings can even exchange their picks.

In terms of getting children to help with chores, consistency is key as well. Let your child know the timeframe he or she is expected to complete their chore within and if they don't, a little consequence is in order. For example, if your child does not complete his or her chore in time to go out, kindly tell them that you were hoping they could go but they can't as they didn't do so. This would work better than permitting them to go all the same as there is a chance that it will become a habit. Children need to be given a set time to do chores to ensure seriousness and dedication on their part. In case your child is swamped with other activities such as schoolwork, you can both work together to plan how they can get their chores done in due time.

It will be more beneficial to make a chore seem more like a fun activity than a task for your child. Think of creative ways you can make doing chores more enjoyable for him or her. You can put on some music for you all to sing along to as you work or have a sort of singing contest where children take turns singing a song loudly from the room they are cleaning. You could even give your child a fun role to encourage them to help out. For example, one way to do this is by appointing him or her as the chef and letting them decide the meal they want to assist with making.

By assigning chores to our children, we help them to learn practical skills for caring for themselves and also contribute to society. They help children to feel capable and independent and allows them to exercise more power and control over their own world. It is also an opportunity for them to contribute in meaningful ways to the home. Giving responsibilities to children make them part of the family because they feel significant when they can contribute with their hard work as well. Although children may not always be excited to do household chores, their contributions make a significant difference in the family and they also help to keep the home running. Since everyone enjoys the privileges in the home, everyone should take part in the responsibilities as well. By learning how to handle their responsibilities, children also pick up vital life skills that will be beneficial to them along the way. Make out time to train them on how to do their responsibilities and let your expectations for them be realistic in relation to their age. With proper encouragement for efforts they make, children will be more excited to repeat these actions. While it can be a struggle to get them to help, being consistent with your expectations and holding them accountable will help them to see chores as necessary activities that can be enjoyed and not as burdens.

Chapter Summary

- Assigning chores to children helps them to grow into emotionally healthy adults and teaches them responsibility.
- Think of fun, creative ways to make your child more interested in helping out at home.
- Children need to know that their input matters too and letting them do chores is one way to do this.
- As house chores involve teamwork, your child learns to view things from another person's perspective and also improves their cooperation skills.

AFTERWORD

As you have reached the end of this book, you now have the needed skills to help your child feel more comfortable with you and also increase their chances of transforming into healthy disciplined adults. Being able to have a relationship that is based on love, mutual respect, and equality with our kids is a gift that should be appreciated. We need to remember that we need to earn our children's respect instead of demanding for it or forcing them to show us respect. By working hand in hand with them, we can create better and more enjoyable relationships for all parties involved. Regardless of what society says or what we are used to, the best kinds of parents are those that are gentle with their kids. By being tough, we only gain our children's fear and not their respect. If you've ever heard the saying that "respect is reciprocal," you would agree that the only way to gain respect is by firstly giving it out.

There's no doubt that it can be tough to try seeing things from a child's point of view all the time and paying attention to their motives instead of their behaviors. While it may not

AFTERWORD

always be easy, the long-lasting results that can come from doing so are incredibly worth it. Remember to be patient with your child and keep in mind that as you're learning along the way, so are they too. By being patient and making the decision to make use of gentle and respectful parenting in all situations, your child will also see the values and be more cooperative.

Never think that it is impossible for your home to have an atmosphere of respect and discipline—in fact, it is much more achievable than you can imagine. With consistency, patience, and by putting in genuine efforts, you too can be a parent to a loving, respectful, and disciplined child. If you have not started doing this already, it isn't too late—your peace of mind will be guaranteed, your home will be a more positive environment and even better, your children will be thankful for it now and in the future. Make the decision to be a gentle and respectful parent toward your child now and get ready to enjoy the blessings that lie therein. Raising well-behaved and happy children is achievable, you only need to make the conscious decision to do so. The best gift we can give to our children is proper training and by doing this, we can be sure that they will grow to love and respect us.

Manufactured by Amazon.ca
Bolton, ON